THE FIVE KEYS TO PERMANENT WEIGHT CONTROL

THE FIVE KEYS TO PERMANENT WEIGHT CONTROL

The Essential Guide for Achieving Your Ideal Weight

Marvin H. Berenson, M.D.

Cove Books
Beverly Hills, California

Cove Books
P.O. Box 11688
Beverly Hills, CA 90213-4688

The Five Keys to Permanent Weight Control
The Essential Guide for Achieving Your Ideal Weight

This book is not intended to be a substitute for medical advice by physicians or other health care professionals. Rather it provides an instructional program for dieting and weight control and is intended to offer information to help readers on their quest for optimal health.

Cover design: Robert Aulicino

Publisher's Cataloging-in-Publication
(Provided by Quality Books, Inc.)

Berenson, Marvin H.
The five keys to permanent weight control : the essential guide for achieving your ideal weight / Marvin H. Berenson. -- 1st ed.
p. cm.
Includes index.
LCCN: 2001118848
ISBN: 0-9700885-2-3

1. Reducing diets. I. Title

RM222.2B47 2002 613.2'5
QBI01-201214

Printed in the United States of America

To Renee, Douglas, and Alex

CONTENTS

ACKNOWLEDGMENTS

No book comes to fruition without the support and encouragement of many people and I want to acknowledge those who helped me.

Above all I want to thank my editor, Mary Embree, who is also a literary consultant and the author of a guide to writing a book, *The Author's Toolkit.* I owe her a debt of gratitude for her in-depth editing and persistent suggestions to improve the format of the book. With her great skill and intuition she guided me to construct a more succinct and readable book than I would have been capable of doing alone. She always seemed to know what required modification, deletion, and reorganization.

I also want to thank the people who willingly offered me suggestions and advice regarding certain aspects of the book. They include Patricia Rosenburg, Dr. Shari Delisle, Donna Dubrow, and Rosalind Glickman, the author of *Optimal Thinking.*

I want to thank Robert Aulicino, my cover designer, for providing me with an outstanding cover and for his ability to create a design that touched my own feelings about the book.

Among my primary supporters were my three children. Renee, whose astute and bottom-line thinking forced me to reflect on issues that needed clarification. Douglas, ever ready with multiple suggestions and seeing beyond the mere words, brought coherence to various issues, and Alex, whose ability to directly focus on any subject helped me rethink and restructure certain aspects of the book.

I am in debt to my many patients who initially helped me develop this program and above all provided me with unlimited support as they wholeheartedly endorsed the five components of the program. Without them this diet program would not exist.

INTRODUCTION

Shortly after I completed my psychiatric and psychoanalytic training, I turned to the study of mental imagery to enhance my artistic interests and explore creativity. I experimented with many types of imagery and felt my personal world opening in ways I had not experienced before. Within a short time I began to use imagery in my private practice to help certain patients overcome negative attitudes and various emotional problems.

The first patients who helped me develop effective imagery techniques were those with psychosomatic disorders such as migraine headaches, abdominal ailments, and various skin conditions. Encouraged by the improvement in many of these patients, I soon applied imagery to the treatment of addictions and compulsive behavior. Imagery exercises proved to be effective for these conditions. I developed imagery programs to assist smokers who wanted to quit and for overweight people who wanted to find a permanent weight control method.

I extended the use of mental imagery to other areas where changing their thinking could help people change their behavior. As before, I first experimented with myself but soon applied it to patients and others who wanted to use this powerful tool. I began to use it as a vehicle to help people develop creativity, improve athletic performance, write stories, and enhance other artistic endeavors. Although my initial purpose was to help my patients overcome symptoms and negative behavior, I realized I had found an effective technique to turn negative beliefs into positive ones. Personal growth was the outcome.

Imagery has been used for hundreds if not thousands of years as a way to explore the inner self and bring forth new ideas that foster personal and social growth. As I became increasingly involved with imagery techniques I began to recognize that no thoughts are sacred and no images are permanent. Life is changeable and in a state of flux. Through imagery and the imagination all thoughts and behavior are open to scrutiny and possible modification.

As my experience with imagery grew I increasingly focused on weight control problems and realized the need to develop a complete diet program. My first overweight patients helped me develop the mental imagery exercises that I came to use as the basis for weight control. Over time I developed the other four components of the diet program, namely, the special way to use water, the positive use of the bathroom scale, exercise, and the stabilization period.

As the program became known, I began to see a variety of overweight people who wanted to achieve their ideal weight and lead a healthier and more vital life. I saw many of them for only a few sessions, teaching them the full diet program, including orienting them to the broad use of imagery.

Over the thirty years that the full program has been in force I have seen hundreds of overweight patients and have come to appreciate the different ways that the five components of the program were used. However, it was the use of imagery that evoked the greatest interest for my patients. For the first time many of them had a tool that not only helped them gain permanent weight control but also offered them creative control over other areas of their lives.

Mental imagery can open doors to your inner world. You will discover unknown areas of yourself. Many of the persons who came to see me to learn about this new diet program became instantaneous imagery devotees. I became caught up in the many ways that imagery was being used by countless patients. I essentially became a mental imagery facilitator.

My conviction of its widespread value for human growth intensified. I became convinced that once a person takes the path to self-growth and they have learned to use imagery for a specific purpose it could be used in other areas. At that point the process is only limited by the individual's imagination.

We're all susceptible to outside influences. Just imagine how a charismatic orator can influence you. Or how a powerful movie can cause you to cry or laugh or feel fear. These experiences don't just go away after the event. They remain with us for varying amounts of time. With imagery and consistent use of the exercises you can sustain changes until finally those changes lead to a new way of behaving and living.

Imagery is powerful but to realize the full potential of the diet program you need to use the other four keys as well. They complement imagery in helping you change your thinking and belief systems and give you greater control over your behavior, including your compulsive eating. Permanent weight control is not only based on what you eat but on why and how you eat. The keys are not just for diet control. They are to help you improve your health and self-esteem and show you how to lead a longer and more vital life.

Being controlled by as tenacious a habit as overeating affects more than your body. It affects your mind. Thus controlling your body is in reality controlling your mind.

Exercise is not only a way to maintain weight control. It should be a part of your plan to live more healthfully. It increases your energy level, both physically and mentally, and gives you greater freedom to indulge in various activities, including sex.

Helping people lose weight extends to helping them live more fully. The mind is the primary key. And the five keys are all directed to the mind in one way or another. The simple act of making a bathroom scale into a friend or psychological assistant, as I call it, is nothing less than a change in one's thinking. A bathroom scale is no longer just a scale.

When I realized that dieting should alternate with non-dieting I conceived the stabilization period as a necessary factor in developing permanent weight control. It seemed so self-evident for dieting that I was unable to understand why it wasn't universally used. But I understood how dieters and those advising them were more concerned with rapid weight loss than with permanency. We have known for years that most dieters gain back the weight they lost. The fact that a person's basal metabolic rate is reduced during prolonged calorie reduction or fasting is not a new discovery. Making stabilization a fundamental part of my diet program seemed obvious and the successful experience of many patients confirmed this.

The stabilization period is also a time for reflection and introspection. It provides an opportunity to examine how thoughts and activities influence eating behavior as well as the tendency to relapse. It is a time to get in touch with yourself as you learn to control your weight.

Believing that you can change yourself is at the heart of this program. If you change your thinking and become empowered to control your behavior then you will be different. You will have control over your actions. Then it's only a small step to changing your life.

CHAPTER ONE

Lifelong Weight Control

Dieting and weight control are fighting words for a large portion of the population. Many diet programs, both new and recycled, offer overweight people a variety of methods to lose weight and stay thin. But few work permanently. Over 90 percent of those who lose weight regain it within the following two years. Most gain the weight back within a year.

Most diet programs do not address all of the elements necessary for permanent weight control. This book focuses on those issues and provides you with the five keys to reaching your ideal weight and maintaining it for the rest of your life. You will learn how you can eat normally, following the guidelines of accepted dietary practices, without worrying about gaining weight. You won't have to buy special foods or limit their variety. And you will improve your physical and emotional health as you lose those unwanted pounds.

Over the past thirty years I have developed a highly successful weight-loss program through working with patients in my clinical practice. They included dieters who had struggled to overcome tenacious eating habits for many years without success and patients who were starting their first diet program. I've also worked with overweight people who faced strong psychological reactions to their obesity and needed to address these issues as part of their diet program. Binge eaters, day-long food nibblers, compulsive overeaters, and women with premenstrual syndrome also sought help with their overeating. Many came, not for psychotherapy, but to spend a few sessions with me to learn about the diet program.

I realized that if my program worked so well for such a wide variety of overweight people, it could work for anyone. *The Five Keys to Permanent Weight Control* is the result of my long and deeply felt commitment to helping people lose weight, improve their health, and maintain their ideal weight permanently.

THE FIVE KEYS

Mental imagery

Well established mental imagery techniques are described to give you the necessary psychological tools to reduce cravings for food and change your thinking and beliefs about eating.

Water

You will learn a specific method of using water to reduce hunger and food intake. It will become a daily tool to help you lose weight. The use of water is a major element in lifelong diet control.

The bathroom scale

You will learn how the daily use of your bathroom scale can help you monitor your progress and keep you on the right path. With the aid of a special one-day water diet, your scale also becomes a psychological assistant. It provides you a way to lose the weight you may have gained the day before. By so doing you will be able to overcome any negative feelings you have about temporary weight gain.

Exercise

You will learn how a special exercise program can permanently increase your metabolic rate and thus allow a greater intake of food without gaining weight. Exercise also enhances cardiovascular health, muscle tone, and self-esteem.

Stabilization

A unique and crucial feature of my weight loss program is the introduction of the stabilization period. This is where you learn to keep the weight off for life. You will learn how to alternate a dieting month with a weight stabilization month. This alternation prevents the body's homeostatic mechanisms from lowering the basal metabolic needs as a person adjusts to a lower intake of food. By not decreasing your basal metabolism you will find that each calorie reduction will provide the same loss of weight. It will be as easy to lose the last ten pounds as the first ten pounds.

The stabilization period provides you with time to gradually adjust to your new weight and body size. Since adjustments are made regularly throughout the program, they diminish the tendency to regain what has been lost. During stabilization you gain a new belief in your ability to eat a normal diet without gaining weight.

These five factors comprise a well-tested and effective program that has been used successfully in my clinical practice by hundreds of overweight people. Many of the ideas I propose may at first seem unusual or certainly very different from what you have learned about dieting. However, they are eminently rational and user-friendly. The program is based on scientific evidence and is consistent with the accepted diet programs of the National Institute of Health (NIH), the American Diabetes Association (ADA), and other medical associations and diet specialists.

Diets go in and out of vogue as our understanding of nutrition changes and new diet medications are developed. Diet recipe books and specially prepared foods that offer you a way of dieting without preparing your own meals contribute to the shifting popularity of diet programs. Many of the diets are quite different from each other which raises the concern that some of the programs may be promoting a less healthy alternative.

If there is a scientific basis for good nutrition, and I believe there is, then all diets can't be equally beneficial. My primary purpose is to offer a diet program that is healthy, that will definitely help you lose weight, and that will give you a new method of permanent weight control. This program teaches you how to change your thinking and maintain your weight loss. It also provides you with a new lifestyle based on an innovative eating paradigm.

You will learn simple techniques to overcome hunger. You will discover how to eliminate any negativity about your weight fluctuations. You will find out what a healthy diet is and how to maintain it. You will find that favorite desserts and occasional splurging will not have any effect on your overall weight.

You will be shown how to effectively change your belief systems about eating and thus overcome forever your compulsive eating habits.

Mental imagery, a technique now widely used to change and improve many areas of thinking and behavior, will become a unique tool that uses your imagination to foster weight management.

Imagery has been used for hundreds of years to change belief systems. More recently it has been used to improve and overcome psychosomatic disorders and other medical conditions. Many world-class athletes maximize their performance with imagery.

Creativity can be stimulated and enhanced. Actors, artists, and writers use imagery to expand their capacity to perform and tell stories. Addictions, including nicotine addiction, have been eliminated with mental imagery. And now you will be able to learn the same imagery techniques to help you finally overcome your eating compulsion.

This book is about more than dieting. It shows you how to have control over your impulses. Through mental imagery another side of your personality will be activated to promote your total well-being. You will learn to empower your mind to change many aspects of your life.

As you learn how to reach your ideal body weight and live a healthy life without constantly worrying about weight and food, you will experience a renewed sense of personal freedom.

In addition to having a healthier and better looking body, consider the other reasons to lose weight.

You Will Increase Your Life Span

Being overweight increases the work of your heart and other body organs and decreases longevity. It has been estimated that over 500,000 Americans die yearly of various illnesses such as heart disease, stroke, hypertension, and diabetes that are related to excessive body weight. Obesity increases the incidence of uterine and breast cancer in women, prostate cancer in men, and colorectal cancer in both sexes. Even small reductions in weight can add years to your life.

You Will Improve Your Health

Osteoarthritis, sleep apnea, gallbladder disease, and endocrine abnormalities leading to irregular menstrual cycles are more common in obesity. Many overweight people tend to exercise less and are more easily fatigued. They engage in less sex, sports, and outdoor activities. The extra body fat requires the heart to increase its output of blood. The additional strain on the heart can lead to increasing cardiac insufficiency and may end in heart failure and an early death.

You Will Increase Your Self-Esteem

This accompanies the improvement in your health and increased self-control. The enhancement in your self-esteem produces a new feeling of vitality, greater productivity, and personal satisfaction. The change in your thinking and behavior leads to permanent weight control and a genuine sense of accomplishment.

Starting a new diet and overcoming previous yo-yo dieting experiences are not necessarily easy. But the rewards of finally having a diet that works and knowing that you're truly changing your way of thinking about eating are many. Once you have gained this kind of mastery you have empowered yourself in ways that will extend far beyond just controlling your weight. You will have a new revitalized sense of self.

The diet can be anything you want it to be as long as you don't exceed your total daily metabolic needs. You can eat any foods you want. There is no need to buy prepared foods. You don't have to count calories or weigh portions. You won't gain weight if you don't exceed your daily need of calories. You maintain weight control through the use of the scale.

Most overweight people should start their diet using all five components of the program. Some of my patients have started with the imagery alone. Only after they felt a sense of mental change did they begin their actual diet. A few patients began their diet using only water, the bathroom scale, and the stabilization period. Later they introduced mental imagery into their personal program.

There are no hard and fixed rules. However, using all five components offer the greatest probability of success. In addition, I suggest that you use a journal in your diet program.

This program gives you the essential tools for dieting and weight management. It explains how to overcome obstacles and psychological issues that interfere with achieving your goal. And it helps you avoid any tendency to relapse.

Changing your thinking is the essential element in making your weight loss permanent. Changing your belief systems changes your life.

CHAPTER TWO

The Psychology of Eating

The relationship between eating and weight gain starts with birth. Newborns must eat to survive and through crying and evidence of inner stress they initiate being fed. Survival is at stake. The need to be loved and nurtured by physical contact and the expression of love is quickly tied to the intake of food. The child takes in the mother's love, caring, and devotion during feeding. Infants who are not held and loved during feeding may become agitated, sickly, unable to keep food down, and even stop eating. The need for love is as important to the nourishment and growth of the infant as food itself.

During the rearing of children many conflicts can develop around feeding. A mother who is not attentive to an infant's needs or is late for feedings or in a bad mood during the feeding period may cause the baby to feel unloved. Such feelings, even when inadvertent, may persist into adulthood and become manifested in eating problems.

Most mothers are very concerned about their infant's needs. A mother's desire to bond with her child is as strong as the child's need to be loved. An infant's well-being and even survival depends on this interaction.

Sibling rivalry may contribute to feelings of rejection, of not being loved, or of feeling second best. Some children, though equally loved, feel deep resentment toward a new baby that enters the family and may never fully overcome the sense of loss of their former position. Food can become the substitute for that feeling of loss.

The loss of a parent during childhood can have a harmful effect on children and leave them with a fear of abandonment. They may be unable to express love for fear that their loved ones will disappear. Physical or sexual abuse can leave the child with feelings of rejection and fearful that the outside world is threatening and unsafe. Any of these experiences can get tied to eating behavior.

Experiences of childhood, no matter what they are, do not necessarily have to be connected to eating or overeating. However, it is always useful to assess the emotions that accompany your overeating. In the chapter on journal use, a number of questions will help you focus on this connection.

Compulsive behavior tends to develop a life of its own as in binge eating or overeating of any kind. Since emotional conflicts and obsessive thoughts contribute to this type of behavior, it is possible to overcome these compulsions by changing your beliefs through imagery. But such strong feelings can also create resistance to change and forestall your gaining the control you seek. Don't overlook this area. It may need to be a focus of your imagery and weight control techniques. Such imagery can be highly effective if you have been able to ascertain what psychological conflicts need to be changed.

Emotional Problems

Many people prefer to ignore psychological problems, seeing them as a sign of weakness or mental instability. Such feelings are understandable. Although our society still tends to place mental illness in the category of unacceptable illnesses there is less stigma than in past years. Having emotional problems is the norm and stems from the variety of conflicts we all face from childhood to our present age. No one is free of conflicts. As we grow up we find ways to compensate, adapt, or hide, or we develop symptoms. Slowly through maturation and insight we change, and eventually many people live a relatively conflict-free existence.

Almost everyone to some degree has difficulties that interfere with his or her life. Whether the real problem is obesity or social phobia or feeling inferior or doubting our intelligence or attractiveness, we suffer from self-doubt and self-criticism. Most of us find ways to adapt or make compromises and learn to live life as well as possible within our limitations. Through personal efforts we sometimes gain insight into our conflicts and learn to change our behavior. We can then find increased satisfaction and a sense of accomplishment.

When obsessive or compulsive behavior controls you, it interferes with your productivity and sense of well-being. Frequently, people are unaware of how much their loss of control affects their life.

Overeating, though not a true addiction like smoking,

has a strong compulsive side that has gained control over the person's mind. In certain ways it is as tenacious and difficult to overcome as the addiction to cigarettes. The dangers of excessive weight are well known but that knowledge doesn't convince people to diet. By accepting that your weight is out of control, you can begin to tackle the underlying negative beliefs that affect many overeaters.

Once you understand the psychological factors that contribute to your overeating you will be able to work toward overcoming them through the use of mental imagery. Mental imagery is not a cure-all for emotional problems but is useful in changing attitudes and behavior that contribute to overeating. Whether depression is a primary cause of your overeating or you get depressed because you are overweight, either way you are depressed. Thus by diminishing your depression you reduce the effect your emotional conflicts have on your diet control. Developing imagery to overcome any negative emotions tends to be very constructive in your weight control program.

CHAPTER THREE

The Ingredients of a Good Diet

Most people who make the effort to control their weight also prefer to eat a healthy diet. They know that weight control is not only about looking better, it is about being healthy. I encourage everyone who is searching for an effective weight control program to learn what comprises a healthy and delicious diet. Only a few salient facts need to be known to eat such a diet.

Many diets, including some you may have tried, are intricately tied to certain foods (grapefruit) or types of food (high protein or low carbohydrates). Although my program is primarily concerned with how you eat, why you eat, and when you eat, I know that eating healthy foods can augment your dietary control and certainly will make you a much healthier person. In developing a lifelong diet you will need to consider what is healthy, what will make your weight control more effective, and what will be enjoyable to eat.

Planning a healthy diet can be gratifying and fun when you know that you have an almost unlimited variety of foods to choose from. You'll find you can include many of your favorite dishes. The only caveat is to try and keep it within established guidelines: 10% to 15% protein, 25% to 30% fat, and 55% to 65% carbohydrates. If you can, restrict your fats to less than 25% and use primarily polyunsaturated and monounsaturated fats.

PROTEINS

Any type of protein you enjoy fits into this category. Fish, especially fish high in omega-3 lipids, such as salmon, tuna, mackerel, and others can be eaten several time a week. Meat, which includes chicken, turkey, beef, lamb, and pork, should be lean and limited to three or four times a week. Dairy products such as milk, cheese, ice cream, and yogurt, preferably low-fat and non-fat varieties, can be eaten in moderation daily. Proteins in legumes, beans, soybean products, and various grains and vegetables can satisfy much of your protein needs. Above all, prepare foods you like and be moderate in your use of fat.

FATS

The types and amount of fat you eat can affect your overall health and cause obesity. Less than one third of your fat intake should be saturated fats, not always easy to accomplish since saturated fats exist in most healthy foods in varying amounts. Milk products, meats, fish, and oils made from grains (soybeans, corn, and others) have some saturated fat. Some foods such as coconut and palm oil are primarily saturated fats. Many desserts are laden with saturated fats. Try to keep your intake of saturated fats under 20 grams per day.

Monounsaturated fats are the healthiest of all fats

and are found in canola oil, olive oil, most nuts, and avocados. Eat even these healthy fats sparingly in order to keep your total fat intake low.

Polyunsaturated fats are also considered relatively healthy and are found in oils, nuts, grains, and fish. As with the monounsaturated fats, be cautious in eating any food that pushes your fat intake over 30% of your diet calories.

CARBOHYDRATES

By comprising 55% to 65% of your caloric dietary needs, carbohydrates become the most prominent part of your food intake. Preference should be given to complex carbohydrates. Refined carbohydrates like white bread and white rice are generally high in simple sugars and are quickly broken down to glucose, the primary sugar that exists in the bloodstream. Sugar in candy, soft drinks, and desserts, which often include corn sweeteners, fructose, honey, and molasses, are likewise quickly broken down to glucose. In a healthy diet you would keep such simple sugars to a minimum.

Eating more complex carbohydrates, generally seen in whole grains such as wheat, oats, corn, rye, and brown rice, as well as in many vegetables and fruits, are the basis of a healthy diet. You should bear in mind that many cereals and breads are not whole grain and may be loaded with sugar. Why not try to use whole grains as one of your staples? They are quite delicious and add fiber, vitamins, and minerals to your diet.

Vegetables are so varied and plentiful you should be able to find many that satisfy both your palate and your nutritional needs. In general, vegetables that are colorful are most nutritious. I like to think of certain vegetables as super foods due to the many compounds that they contain, such as antioxidants, that protect us from cancer and other serious illnesses. They include broccoli, spinach, tomatoes, carrots, sweet potatoes, yams, kale, peppers (especially red peppers), and dark green leafy vegetables like romaine lettuce. Other less widely used vegetables that are both healthy and tasty are Brussels sprouts, cauliflower, asparagus, garlic, mustard greens, and Swiss chard.

Fruits are also high on the list of healthy foods and should be a part of your daily diet. There are also a number of super fruits based on their high level of phytochemicals, the plant chemicals that improve our level of health. In general, fruits with the deepest and brightest colors are the ones to eat. They include most berries, like strawberries, blueberries, and blackberries; also melons, especially cantaloupe, Crenshaw, honeydew, and watermelon; and oranges, mangos, plums, cherries, and papayas. Apples and bananas, though not highly colored, contain many nutrients.

Therefore, as you plan your diet each day try to include as many whole grains, fruits, and vegetables as possible. They are all high in the micronutrients, including vitamins, minerals, fiber, and phytochemicals that confer good health on us. They provide most of the antioxidants we need to neutralize the free radicals that float in our bloodstream. They also help regulate many bodily functions.

FIBER

Fiber, the indigestible part of food, comes in two forms. The insoluble form increases the rate of food moving through the intestinal tract and adds to stool bulk. The soluble form, which can be dissolved in water, binds bile acids and cholesterol and may help lower blood cholesterol. Both types are found in whole grains, fruits, vegetables, nuts, and seeds. A healthy, moderate carbohydrate diet will assure the dieter of the thirty grams of fiber a day that I recommend. Fiber may help protect us from a variety of conditions, such as irritable bowel syndrome, diverticulitis, and colon cancer.

VITAMINS AND MINERALS

Do you need extra vitamins and minerals if you eat a healthy diet? Deficiency diseases are now relatively rare in our society. However, over half the population uses vitamin and mineral supplements. In addition, most essential vitamins and minerals are added to a variety of foods, supplementing the amounts naturally found in them. In general, those eating a healthy diet do not need most supplements. However, for those who feel more comfortable using supplements or whose diet may be lacking high levels of micronutrients I do have several recommendations.

The only vitamins that you need to add to the amounts normally supplied by foods are vitamin C and vitamin E, both essential antioxidants. The recommended dietary allowance (RDA) for vitamin C is 60 mg and 30 IU for vitamin E. Due to the importance of these two vitamins in a variety of stress-related conditions and in reducing the amount of free radicals in the blood, I recommend more than that. I believe you should supplement your diet with 250 mg of vitamin C and 400 IU of vitamin E a day.

The vitamin B complex present in grains, vegetables, and fruits has a number of essential vitamins that may be supplemented by a B complex tablet that includes B_6, B_{12}, and 400 micrograms of folic acid. Folic acid is particularly recommended for pregnant women and those who want to become pregnant. Deficiencies may cause neural tube defects in fetuses during the first months of pregnancy. Vitamins B_6 and B_{12} regulate the blood level of homocystein, a risk factor in coronary artery disease. Beta-carotene, another important antioxidant, will most likely be supplied in a healthy diet.

Dieters who sharply curtail their food intake over a long period of time may benefit from taking supplements in the form of a multivitamin and mineral tablet.

As with most vitamins, minerals are also added to many foods and occur naturally in a variety of foods, especially vegetables, fruits, and whole grains. Certain minerals, such as iron, are abundant in meats, beans, fruits, and green vegetables such as broccoli. Unless you have an iron deficiency disorder there is no need to supplement your food with iron.

Calcium is an essential ingredient in bone formation. It helps to prevent osteoporosis, facilitates nerve, muscle, kidney, and cardiac functioning, and is not adequately supplied by many diets. Dairy products, certain fish such as sardines, and some leafy green vegetables supply calcium. Also, calcium is frequently added to a variety of foods, including certain cereals, orange and other fruit juices, and frozen yogurt. It has been recommended that all adults have 1,200 to 1,500 mg of calcium a day. If your diet does not supply this amount you should consider taking a daily calcium supplement.

Selenium is another important mineral in the antioxidant defense system and although it occurs in various plants and nuts the amount is not constant. Daily supplementation of selenium should be considered. The amount I recommend is 100 to 200 micrograms a day.

Although my program does not require that you become familiar with the vitamin and minerals in foods or the amount of calories in common servings of foods, such knowledge simplifies your preparation of a healthy diet. Eating large amounts of the super vegetables and fruits each day will fulfill most of your vitamin and mineral requirements.

You can eat anything you want as long as your calorie intake does not exceed your daily metabolic needs. However, you should strive to eat a healthy diet. I adhere to the dietary recommendations of the National Institute of Health, the American Diabetes Association, and the American Dietetic Association. As attaining permanent weight control is your goal, select whatever dietary approach you feel comfortable with.

I suggest that you follow the guidelines developed jointly by the United States Department of Agriculture (USDA) and the Department of Health and Human Services (HHS). These guidelines came after years of study, clinical evaluation, and measuring the overall health of people of all ages. They represent the current advice of nutrition scientists and are followed by most nutrition experts and health institutions.

GUIDELINES OF THE USDA AND HHS

Eat a variety of foods to get the energy, protein, vitamins, minerals, and fiber you need for good health.

Balance the food you eat with physical activity. Maintain or improve your weight to reduce your chances of having high blood pressure, heart disease, a stroke, certain cancers, and the most common kind of diabetes.

Choose a diet with plenty of grain products, vegetables, and fruits that provide needed vitamins, minerals, fiber, and complex carbohydrates, and can help you lower your intake of fat.

Choose a diet low in fat, saturated fat, and cholesterol to reduce your risk of heart attack and certain types of cancer and to help you maintain a healthy weight. Especially reduce your intake of saturated fat.

Choose a diet moderate in sugars. A diet with lots of sugars has too many calories and too few nutrients for most people and can contribute to tooth decay.

Choose a diet moderate in salt and sodium to help reduce your risk of high blood pressure.

If you drink alcoholic beverages, do so in moderation. Alcoholic beverages supply calories but little or no nutrients. Drinking alcohol is also the cause of many health problems and accidents and can lead to addiction.

It is useful to become acquainted with the physical size of what you eat in terms of its caloric value. You should eat a variety of foods to get the nutrients you need and the right amount of calories to maintain healthy weight.

The USDA recommends six to eleven servings from the bread, cereal, rice, and pasta group, three to five servings of vegetables, and two to three of fruits. They suggest two to three servings from the milk group which includes yogurt and cheese, and two to three servings from the group that includes meat, fish, poultry, beans, eggs, and nuts. They emphasize going easy on fats, oils, and sweets.

WHAT COUNTS AS ONE SERVING?

If you eat a large portion, count it as more than one serving. For example, a dinner portion of spaghetti may count as two or three servings of pasta.

Try to pick foods with the lowest amount of fat. No specific serving size is given for the fats, oils, and sweets group because the message is *use sparingly*. Be sure to eat at least the minimal number of servings from the five major food groups. The following are one-serving sizes.

Milk, yogurt, and cheese group

1 cup of milk or yogurt
1½ ounces of natural cheese
2 ounces of processed cheese

Meat, poultry, fish, beans, eggs, and nuts

2 to 3 ounces of lean meat, poultry, or fish
½ cup of beans
one egg
2 tablespoons of peanut butter

Vegetables

one cup of raw leafy vegetables

½ cup of other vegetables, cooked or raw
¾ cup of vegetable juice

Fruits

one medium apple, banana, or orange
½ cup chopped, cooked, or canned fruit
¾ cup of fruit juice

Bread, cereal, rice, and pasta

one slice of bread
one ounce of ready-to-eat cereal
½ cup of cooked cereal, rice, or pasta

Eating a nutritionally adequate diet contributes to your ability to maintain weight control. It enhances your developing a positive attitude toward yourself independent of your weight and actually increases motivation to maintain normal weight. It will help you live a healthier and more vital life at whatever weight you are.

MEASURING PORTION SIZE

Despite having the information provided by the USDA available, I realize that most people do not have the interest or motivation to learn what constitutes a measured portion of food and its calorie count. It's not easy to do. Many things influence the amount of calories in foods. For example, consider the following. What is a medium size apple or banana? An apple can be 75 or 150 calories. Is your tablespoon a true tablespoon in size? Bread comes in different sizes. Some slices are as low as 40 calories. Some as high as 100 calories. Some rolls can be 200 or 300 calories. How many calories are in a handful of almonds or peanuts or in one almond or one peanut? And do people count almonds or peanuts one by one?

Judging the size of a portion of fish or meat isn't easy. You can be off by 100%. And can you tell how many tablespoons of sauce are in your pasta dish? If it's a fat-laden sauce you can be off by several hundred calories. Many sauces, such as Alfredo sauce, have a large amount of fat. Pure oil is 120 calories per tablespoon. Many sauces approach that caloric value. A single tablespoon of sauce in a large bowl of pasta would hardly be noticed. So how many tablespoons are in it? It is helpful to practice measuring portion size and calories in all your foods, but caution and carefulness become the watchwords when judging portion sizes.

Eating in restaurants makes it quite difficult to know what ingredients are in the food set before you. Fats can be hidden in the preparation of the vegetables, meats, or sauces. Several glasses of wine that you may not ordinarily drink during home meals, and enticing desserts can add many calories. People on diets try to avoid any obviously fattening food and for brief periods of time their motivation and discipline aid this control. But, as is well known, maintaining the control tends to falter for the many reasons still to be discussed.

CHAPTER FOUR

Sizing Yourself Up

What is the relationship of body size and being overweight? The question is not simple for it involves the concept of body image. We tend to react to our body size by comparing it to our desired body image, which is frequently idealized. The determination of body image reflects cultural and social norms, ethnic attitudes, age, identification with idealized celebrities, childhood experiences with eating, and personal feelings about one's body size.

Dieting to reach a desired and realistic body size is at the heart of most diet programs. Understanding the accepted norms for body size and its relationship to weight is therefore useful in gauging how realistic your weight loss goal is. The guidelines established by the National Heart, Lung and Blood Institute (NHLBI), a part of the National Institute of Health (NIH) are followed by most diet programs. For some overweight people knowing the statistics regarding the relation of body size and body weight is important. For others it isn't. However, being overweight has a significant effect on health and longevity and information that helps you lose weight permanently is useful.

METHODS OF MEASURING BODY FAT

The Body Mass Index (BMI)

The BMI has become the preferable method to determine whether a person is overweight. The system uses body fat and not body weight as its baseline guide. The five BMI categories—underweight, healthy weight, overweight, obesity, and extreme obesity—are based on the government's 1998 "Clinical Guidelines on the Identification, Evaluation, and Treatment of Overweight and Obesity in Adults." Since the index is a good measure of fatness it can help you identify your risk of developing a variety of weight-related illnesses, such as Type 2 diabetes, heart disease, high blood pressure, stroke, and osteoarthritis. It applies to men and women.

Formula to determine your BMI

Multiply your weight in pounds by 704.5
Multiply your height by your height in inches
Divide the first result by the second

Example

If you're 5' 5" and weigh 150 pounds:
150 x 704.5 = 105,675
65 x 65 = 4,225
105,675 divided by 4,225 = 25

Formula for the metric system

Multiply your weight in kilograms by 10,000
Multiply your height by your height in centimeters
Divide the first result by the second

Example

If you're 165 cm and weigh 66 kg:
66 x 10,000 = 660,000
165 x 165 = 27,225
660,000 divided by 27,225 = 24.24

THE NHLBI GUIDELINES

BMI	5'5"	5'10"
Underweight		
18.5 or less	Under 110 lbs.	Under 129 lbs.
Healthy weight		
18.5 to 25	111 to 149 lbs.	130 to 173 lbs.
Overweight		
25 to 30	150 to 179 lbs.	174 to 208 lbs.
Obese		
30 to 40	180 to 239 lbs.	209 to 277 lbs.
Extreme obesity		
40 and over	240 lbs. and up	278 lbs. and up

The BMI guidelines are not accurate for heavily muscled people such as athletes, bodybuilders, and weightlifters.

Waist to hip ratio

This determines the amount of fat in the abdominal and hips area. A person measures the circumference of the waist at its smallest point and the circumference of the hips at their widest point. The ratio of waist to hip is then calculated. The recommended ratio for women is less than 0.80. For men the ratio is 0.95 or lower. This ratio distinguishes persons who carry most of their excess fat in the abdominal area, sometimes known as the "apples" from those who carry their excess fat around the hips and buttocks, known as the "pears."

This calculation has considerable practical value since the accumulation of fat in the abdomen causing a higher waist/hip ratio is associated with higher risk for cardiovascular disease. Thus there is an urgent need for overweight people in the "apple" category to lose weight.

Waist measurement

An increasing number of medical professionals believe that measuring your waist alone is a better indication of your abdominal fat than the waist/hip ratio. For women a waist measurement of over 35 inches (88 centimeters) and for men over 40 inches (102 centimeters) puts them at higher risk for heart disease and diabetes than someone with lower measurements. This increased danger is accentuated when other risk factors such as smoking, excessive drinking, diabetes, family history of heart disease, high blood pressure, and a sedentary lifestyle are present.

Abdominal fat cells tend to be more active in absorbing fat and then releasing the fat back into the bloodstream. The increased blood fat causes the liver to make more fat-containing particles that clog the arteries causing atherosclerosis which leads to coronary artery disease. Fortunately, the fat distributed in the abdominal area is easier to get rid of by dieting than the fat in many other areas of the body.

The recommended optimal body fat percentages for men are 11% to 17%. Over 20% body fat is considered obesity. For women the optimal body fat is 19% to 22%, with 23% to 30% considered moderate and over 30% obesity. In general, specific statistics on one's body fat, though of interest, tells less than the BMI. The correlation of the BMI and actual body fat percentages is high.

BODY SIZE VERSUS BODY IMAGE

Knowing the relationship of your height and weight, as well as your body mass and body fat percentage may propel you to consider dieting for the sake of your health, but they have little to do with how you feel about your body. Most of us tend to separate health concerns from our feelings of self-esteem when we regard our body. The health danger of being overweight has rarely convinced people to establish a healthy diet. Most overweight people readily admit that feeling heavy has less to do with excess weight than with their mental image and the effect it has on their physical activities and relationships. An active runner, for example, would feel that any excess weight interferes with his running ability. An actress could assume that being even slightly overweight would jeopardize her career. Most people believe that being overweight makes them less desirable to their spouse or lover.

The weight that triggers a negative body image can be any amount over what the individual personally considers proper weight. Thus a man of 5' 10" who weighs between 150 and 160 pounds may feel overweight or underweight even though he's within a healthy range. It depends on his body image, his general level of self-esteem, his perception of his sex appeal, and his sense of acceptance socially and professionally. His feelings about his body image are also related to his age and the presence of physical abnormalities. Psychological factors such as self-doubt, depression, and feeling unloved may affect his reaction to his body size.

Negative reactions toward overweight women tend to be greater that for overweight men. Accordingly, women in our society face a greater challenge than men in maintaining a realistic and comfortable feeling about their body size.

The BMI, as well as other height/weight tables in current use, create their own problems by the wide range of acceptable body weights for a particular height. For example, a woman 5' 5" tall, using the NHLBI guidelines, can weigh between 111 and 149 pounds and be considered within a normal healthy range. Yet, she will feel quite different at 111 pounds than she will at 149 pounds. Such a wide disparity in weights is partly dependent on frame size. However this tends to do little for most women's assessment of their body image.

It is difficult to reassure her that she looks fine at a weight she believes is too heavy for her body. If her reaction to her body image is intense, even if she knows that her reaction is distorted, she may suffer enormously. Some women, despite being within the accepted healthy weight range, feel continuously embarrassed and want to hide their bodies.

Many overweight women have come to accept

their body size and do not suffer a loss of self-esteem. Some will go on diets more for health improvements than for a need to feel more attractive.

What does all this have to do with weight control? Everything. For too long our society has been entranced by the silhouettes of movie stars, professional models, and star athletes to the detriment of one's personal self. Many people create a specific mental picture of a body type that would be far removed from their potential body size and appearance even after effective dieting.

To diet successfully it is important that you carefully appraise your attitudes about your current figure and any tendency you have toward idealization. If, during your diet, your actual body appearance differs from your idealized figure, you could become disappointed and stop dieting. Idealized images rarely take into account differences in body frame, percentage of muscle versus fat, and how the fat is distributed throughout the body. You need to reassess your body image in terms of your actual physical shape and what may be attainable in a successful diet program.

Examining areas of self-doubt and inferiority feelings may assist you in making this change. Although you want to develop and maintain a body size consistent with your health, there is a wide range of such body sizes for your height.

Self-acceptance is a primary requirement for proper weight control. You need to accept your body as it gradually changes during your diet and recognize all the benefits that come with weight loss. Then, as you reach your desired body size you will have learned to embrace and enjoy your real body.

CHAPTER FIVE

Other Factors in Dieting

Genetics also play a part in body size, fat distribution, metabolic rates, and the potential to become diabetic. They must be taken into consideration in establishing a realistic body image and developing your diet program. Most genetic factors create the potential or predisposition for something to happen.

GENETICS AND OBESITY

You don't have to become obese just because it runs in your family. Except in unusual circumstances, the effects of most genetic factors can be partly or even completely overcome by increased motivation and discipline. The use of mental imagery can counter genetic influences and help overcome many handicaps by changing belief systems about your body. Many handicaps can be overcome by changing belief systems about your body and sense of self.

In recent years a number of breakthroughs in the genetics of obesity have given us hope that someday a way will be found to alter defective genes in the obese. At least five different genes are now known to influence body weight. In a paper, *The Genetics of Obesity*, Dr. Jules Hirsch of Rockefeller University and Dr. Rudolph Leibel of Columbia University describe the differences in the adipose tissue of the obese who have lost weight and the adipose tissue of the non-obese. There is a distinctive difference in cellular architecture implying a fundamental difference in fat deposits in markedly overweight people. The significance of this difference remains unknown. However, it does appear to validate many obese people's belief that they metabolize and utilize food differently from others. It is not clear what part other causes may play in changing the cellular architecture of adipose tissue.

The authors emphasize the complexity of studying the biology of obesity and the need to take into account behavior and developmental effects as well as genetic influences. That genetic factors play an important role in obesity is no longer questioned. Studies of obesity in twins, in families, and in adopted children and their parents imply that genetic factors influence obesity. Nevertheless, the authors stress that obesity is absolutely dependent on the availability of sufficient food and on its consumption. We need to rely on diet and weight control to counteract any genetic predisposition that individuals may have.

A newly discovered hormone, leptin, identified in mice and humans, reduced the body weight in mice by 30% after just two weeks of treatment, reported Drs. Jeffrey Friedman and Stephen K. Burley of Rockefeller University. They indicate that leptin is a hormone that regulates body weight by signaling the brain of the amount of fat stored. They found that synthetic versions of mouse and human leptin decreased the body weight of mice by reducing their food intake and increasing their energy output.

The instructions to make leptin are carried by a gene that is defective in the obese mouse. Defects in the gene called *ob* causes the cessation of leptin production in the mouse and results in massive obesity similar to obesity in humans. The signal to stop eating that normally comes from the adipose tissue is not transmitted to the hypothalamus in the brain. It becomes clear that obese persons who do not produce leptin must find another way to transmit a signal to the brain that they have eaten enough.

Considering all the ways that the brain is signaled that enough food has been eaten, it is uncertain what part leptin signals play in people feeling satiated from eating. Further study should show whether humans respond with massive obesity when leptin production is stopped.

Another kind of obese mouse has a different defective gene called diabetes (*db*) and may have levels of leptin ten times greater than normal. The *db* mice are thought to have a defective leptin receptor system and thus can't receive cellular signals. It's similar to having a high level of insulin that has little effect on blood sugar, giving rise to insulin resistant (Type 2) diabetes.

The genetic mechanisms that contribute to obesity in certain people and tend to run in families include metabolic, biochemical, physiological, and endocrine factors. If you believe that such factors add to your weight control difficulties, be aware that they do not prevent you from losing weight but may require greater effort and time. Ultimately, weight loss is strictly a function of calorie intake and calorie utilization. If you can reduce your calorie intake sufficiently and maintain the reduction long enough you will lose weight.

Endocrine Factors During Menstrual Cycle

Normal hormone fluctuations in women during their menstrual cycles frequently cause water retention and temporary weight gain. However, some women who develop premenstrual syndrome (PMS) tend to periodically retain more fluid than normal. Frequently, they become depressed and discouraged and begin to overeat. Thus what begins as a temporary overweight condition due to water retention may develop into permanent weight gain.

Fluctuations in estrogen and progesterone affect salt and water retention and are generally associated with premenstrual symptoms. At times this weight gain cycle is intensified by other symptoms of premenstrual tension, including emotional instability, agitation, depression, loss of control, irritability, and self-deprecation. These reactions can significantly add to the urgency to overeat, thus increasing the degree of weight gain during the month.

The overeating tends to occur when the hormone changes are most apparent; namely, the few days to a week before the menstrual period and often during the period. With the start of a new cycle, the PMS symptoms disappear and weight gain is reversed but often not completely. When the next PMS period begins the woman is already upset as she tries to cope with the small weight gain sustained the previous month. If the pattern repeats month after month there will be a spiraling cycle of monthly increments of weight gain.

In addition to whatever treatment a woman is using for her PMS, she should try to limit her salt intake and continue her daily use of water for diet control. By adding more water than usual each day that she has premenstrual symptoms there will eventually be a diuresis. The increased urine excretion usually occurs at the end of the menstrual period. Her weight should quickly return to normal. The use of the water differs somewhat in this particular situation since I'm recommending that extra water be taken each day during the PMS period.

All women suffering from PMS, including those receiving medical treatment for their PMS, should consult with their physician about treating their water retention and edema with extra water. Some women are being treated with diuretics, oral contraceptives, and tranquilizers for nervousness. They should make certain that the regimen of extra water is not in conflict with their other treatment. My personal clinical experience has not shown any negative effects in women with PMS and in many cases it appeared to help relieve their symptoms.

Other dietary needs and weight control techniques should not be affected by the monthly endocrine changes in women. However, there is one caution to keep in mind. If there is any unusual fluid retention or excretion that does not seem related to endocrine factors, salt, or water intake, a medical evaluation is in order. Conditions as diverse as congestive heart failure, diabetes, and kidney disease should be ruled out.

Dr. Neal D. Barnard and a team of researchers at Georgetown School of Medicine studied 33 women with moderate to severe PMS using a low-fat (less than

10% fat but high in omega-3 fatty acids) vegetarian diet. They found that the diet significantly reduced water retention and weight gain as well as menstrual pain, both in terms of intensity and duration. Women on the diet also had improved concentration and less emotional and behavioral symptoms.

If you are a woman with severe PMS you may wish to consider radically reducing your fat intake two or three days before the expected onset of symptoms. If you find improvement in your symptoms, I suggest your continuing it throughout the PMS period. During this time maintain the same calorie input that you arrived at for your general diet period. Severe PMS that can last seven to ten days is very incapacitating and it's worth attempting reasonable dietary approaches to determine if diet can help reduce symptoms. Again this should be discussed with your personal physician for guidance and advice.

HOW EMOTIONS INFLUENCE WEIGHT CONTROL

Overeating is common during periods of depression, sexual frustration, loneliness, financial setbacks, anxiety, marital strife, work or job stress, and rejection by loved ones. Frequently, childhood conflicts remain unresolved and later in life become a contributor, sometimes unconsciously, to overeating. Traumatic experiences such as the loss of a loved one, sexual or physical abuse, or excessive ridicule by other children, siblings and parents can leave emotional scars that later resurface in overeating.

More and more children are becoming obese as they struggle to resolve issues of loss, rejection, inferiority feelings, and increased stress when pushed beyond their capacities. Unable to overcome their growing emotional problems they resort to food to reduce their suffering. As they overeat and gain weight they begin to suffer from a poor body image.

Children are highly sensitive to feelings of being different. Difference often means being unaccepted. Food becomes the substitute and soon the vicious cycle of neediness and poor body image leads to more and more eating. The cycle is often accentuated by their identifying with overweight or obese parents, many of whom talk openly about their own struggles with weight. The rise in Type 2 diabetes in children is partly due to the widespread practice of overeating to attempt to resolve emotional problems. Very similar problems develop in adolescence and frequently parallel childhood patterns.

All overweight adults should attempt to evaluate their childhood and adolescence to try to discover how their past may be involved with their current overeating.

Understanding how emotional problems can interfere with weight control can enhance your ability to change your thinking and beliefs about overeating.

LOVE AND FOOD

Much has been written about the connection between the wish to be loved and the displacement of that wish to food. Loss of love leads to feelings of emptiness and depression. To fill the emptiness, some people eat and feel better. It's almost as though they have been loved. When they again feel unloved they eat again and once more feel better. Soon a third and then a fourth episode occur. This sets up an increasingly tenacious belief that food can replace love and a vicious cycle has evolved.

Complications soon begin. The overeating causes obesity and they feel increasingly less desirable and less loved. Eating is necessary to feel better, to be filled up and feel loved. These feelings are often not conscious. Only the compulsion to eat is felt and known. But an underlying depression has set in, often disguised by the overeating. If self-doubt and feelings of inferiority intensify, these people can withdraw into continual eating to try to ward off awareness of the depression.

Other emotions can enter the picture. Guilt over their inability to control their weight, anger at themselves, and possibly anger at loved ones who show concern about the increased weight can begin to play a part. At times, obsessive fear of the complications of obesity becomes another way to punish themselves for overeating.

Even though such a compulsive pattern may make the weight control program more difficult to use, it does not in itself prevent the program from working.

A number of mental imagery techniques described later are directed to this problem and frequently help to overcome the feelings of inferiority and being unloved.

CHAPTER SIX

Diet Programs and Health Concerns

A brief overview of some of the current popular diet programs will give you the background to help you understand how various diets work. It will provide you with the perspective to better understand what this weight control program offers and how it differs from other diets.

Many programs advocate a low carbohydrate, high protein, and moderate to high fat diet. Such diets include the New Robert Atkins Diet, Barry Sears' The Zone diet, Protein Power, Sugar Busters, Lick the Sugar Habit, and many others. Such diets not only advocate low levels of carbohydrate intake but also actually prohibit certain types of carbohydrates, notably those high on the glycemic index.

THE GLYCEMIC INDEX (GI)

In recent years the GI has become a popular means of determining the types of carbohydrates that are acceptable for the various low carbohydrate diets. Restricting the intake of certain highly nutritious foods based on its position on the GI has aroused much controversy.

The GI measures the rate of absorption and digestion of carbohydrates and the speed of conversion into blood glucose. All foods that contain carbohydrates can be measured and compared to all others based on time and the rate that blood glucose levels increase. The GI ranges from under 10 to over 100. Foods with a GI under 55 that cause a very small elevation of blood glucose are considered healthy. Those between 55 to 70 are acceptable, but somewhat less so, and those over 70 unhealthy. The GI is by no means fully accepted in scientific circles and many dietitians and doctors doubt its validity or usefulness.

Nevertheless, the GI has been widely used to measure the influence that carbohydrate absorption has on the amount of insulin in the blood. It is now generally acknowledged that a rapid increase of blood sugar does increase the output of insulin from the pancreas. A high insulin level allegedly influences the body to convert the glucose into fat, which is stored in the body rather than used as energy. Thus by reducing the amount of all carbohydrates eaten, and especially those that rapidly convert to glucose, you theoretically prevent fat from accumulating in the body.

Is such a theory valid? Various clinical studies indicate that this series of events does take place but it is by no means a simple matter. Other dietary factors contribute to the rapid digestion of simple (all sugars) and complex (starches) carbohydrates. The amount of fiber in the diet determines how rapidly the food moves through the intestinal tract and thus partly controls the rate and the amount of absorption in a given time period. The less fiber the more rapid the absorption and the higher the blood glucose is elevated. This in turn affects the amount of insulin released by the pancreas.

Preparation of the Food

Food preparation contributes to the rate of breakdown and digestion within the intestinal tract. The rate of digestion depends on how food is eaten—sautéed, grilled, boiled, or raw. Carbohydrates combined with fat are absorbed more slowly. Therefore the rate partly depends on the percentage of fat eaten. Foods that are fried differ in their rate of digestion and absorption from other methods of preparation. Mixing foods that are both high and low on the glycemic index also alters the absorption rate.

Simple and Complex Carbohydrates

The type of simple sugar in the food being eaten also plays a part. Foods that have glucose as their primary sugar, such as white bread, grains, and pastas are generally absorbed faster and go directly into the bloodstream. Foods that contain fructose found in fruits and vegetables, and galactose found in dairy products, are absorbed more slowly and must be broken down by the liver before entering the bloodstream as glucose. Also the relative amount of simple to complex carbohydrates plays a part in how rapidly a specific food is absorbed. Even the manner of eating, whether one eats rapidly or slowly plays a part in absorption and thus how fast the blood glucose is elevated.

Insulin

Insulin is elevated temporarily whenever we eat any carbohydrates. Excessive elevation of insulin has detrimental effects on the body in addition to its role in the formation of fat deposits and should be avoided, if possible. But I want to emphasize that normal or even a steep elevation of insulin would not cause any fat storage if the calorie intake was not more than what the body required on a daily basis.

The current preoccupation with the glycemic index and the different rates of carbohydrate absorption have made us forget that fat is not laid down in body tissues if a person does not overeat. No one, no matter what their weight, will increase body fat content if they only eat the number of calories required by their metabolism. People do not gain or lose fat deposits if their weight doesn't fluctuate.

CALORIE LIMITATION

It's not the type of food you eat but the excessive calorie input that causes weight gain. Whether the food contains a predominance of carbohydrates, or fat, or protein, it's the excessive calories and only the excessive calories that are converted into fat. If weight is gained it is gained as fat, unless you are actively engaged in a muscle building exercise program. The rate of absorption of carbohydrates, unless there are excessive calories involved, will not increase body fat. Even those engaged in muscle building exercises will add fat to their body if their calorie input is greater than their needs.

TYPE 2 DIABETES

Another major reason to avoid overeating and causing an elevation of insulin is the potential development of Type 2 diabetes, sometimes called adult-onset or insulin-resistant diabetes. Much of our concern about the amount of carbohydrates we eat and the rapidity of absorption is related to the prospect of developing diabetes. The danger of developing resistance to elevated insulin levels is not high unless one is obese or continues to have rapid swings in food intake and subsequent weight changes.

However, there has been an increase in Type 2 diabetes in both obese adults and children. As Americans have become increasingly overweight, the danger of developing diabetes has increased. The loss of sensitivity to the regulating properties of insulin and the development of insulin resistance occurs slowly. Eventually such resistance, if not overcome, can lead to Type 2 diabetes where hyperglycemia or high blood sugar develops.

The diet recommended by the American Diabetes Association (ADA) comprises low fat, moderate protein, and moderate to high carbohydrates, primarily limited to beans, vegetables, fruits, and grains. The ADA does not distinguish carbohydrates based on the glycemic index but rather on types of foods, emphasizing natural and unrefined foods. Many natural foods, including potatoes, corn, raisins, and others high on the glycemic index that are especially prone to such easy conversion to glucose would not be eliminated by the ADA.

To avoid excessive swings in insulin levels, you should avoid foods with a predominance of simple sugars, such as desserts and products with refined sugars. This is especially true for obese and inactive people. Sixteen million overweight people are estimated to have diabetes and 90% to 95% are Type 2. Most people who actually develop Type 2 diabetes can control and even reverse it through a proper diet, eliminating obesity, developing an exercise program, and stopping smoking.

HIGH PROTEIN INTAKE

Another part of many low carbohydrate diets is the high protein intake that is promoted as a key element in weight loss. Perhaps the best known of the very high protein diets is the Atkins diet. Dr. Robert Atkins believes that carbohydrates are primarily responsible for weight gain and thus advocates a severely restricted carbohydrate intake of 15 to 60 grams a day. Considering that the percentage of carbohydrates in a standard 2,000-calorie diet is 55% to 60% carbohydrates (275-300 grams/day), Dr. Atkins' recommendations are extremely low. He feels that carbohydrates cause excessive insulin production that converts glucose to fat. Along with this restriction of carbohydrates he allows an unlimited consumption of protein and fat.

Dr. Atkins has suggested that his diet works by forcing the body to "burn" stored body fat through a process of dietary ketosis, an alternative energy source. Eating high levels of protein and fat serves two purposes, he believes. Dieters feel satiated by the unlimited protein and fat they eat and thus do not snack on carbohydrates. Also, due to the high protein intake, muscle is not burned for energy. He stresses the need of keeping total calorie input below metabolic needs.

A number of concerns arise with this diet. Eating high levels of fat, especially saturated fat, may be particularly dangerous to those with heart disease. The lack of ready energy from glucose when exercising may give rise to muscle fatigue. Unlimited protein intake may affect the kidneys, increase the risk of osteoporosis, increase calcium loss, and put an excessive burden on the liver, which could be harmful to those with liver disease. Dr Atkins does advocate supplements to avoid nutritional deficiencies but it is difficult to replace the vast array of nutritional benefits from the missing vegetables and fruits.

Another prominent diet program with a high protein intake is The Zone diet devised by Dr. Barry Sears. However, Dr. Sears does not advocate eating unlimited protein. His controlled diet demands exactly 30% proteins, which is still high compared to levels recommended by the NIH and the ADA, and includes three meals of 500 calories each plus two snacks of 100 calories a day. For most people, a diet of only 1,700 calories a day would cause weight loss. All the protein, fat, and carbohydrates in a calorie restrictive diet would be broken down to provide the energy needed to run the body, which includes cell replacement.

An inducement to use the Zone Diet is "entering the Zone." The Zone is a mystical state that, Barry Sears alleges, you go into by eating a diet in the precisely measured proportion of 40% carbohydrates, 30% protein, and 30% fat. Dr. Sears claims this leads to stable insulin levels, giving rise to this special state of mind. He feels it is a part of optimum health, the attainment of a sense of well-being, and an almost transcendent state where the mind is relaxed yet has "exquisite focus." Dr. Sears rightly points out that there are many other ways, such as athletics, meditation, breathing exercises, and visualization that people have used to enter this state of mind. However, could this actually happen from eating an exactly measured proportion of the three dietary components in his diet?

Dr. Sears believes that the Zone is a metabolic state in which the body works at "peak efficiency" and that such a state of mind is most likely to be attained through the use of his special diet. Apparently some people who successfully lose weight, even if temporarily, using that exact proportion of fat, protein, and carbohydrates experience a mental change much as Sears described. Many people who become involved in a special diet movement, as The Zone, will develop a sense of elation or well-being through identification with the movement. How much of this mental change is due to the special diet is not clear. Unfortunately, many people who eventually discontinue the diet and find their weight fluctuating or who get past the initial euphoria of being part of a diet movement lose that special sense of excitement.

In 1990 Mihaly Csikszentmihaly wrote an enlightening and informative book called *Flow: The Psychology of Optimal Experience* in which he describes a similar type of mental change. Through a conscious effort in changing and expanding one's relationship to self, nature, work, sex, physical activities, thought processes, and solitude—in other words, all aspects of life—flow can be achieved. A person would then enter a near transcendent state where focus, alertness, joy, and inner satisfaction exist almost continuously. He does not introduce dietary changes as essential to reaching such a mental state. He explains how a person can achieve maximum efficiency and creative productiveness where the body and mind are united in this optimal condition of living and being.

Practitioners of Yoga and various forms of meditation also claim that such states of mind can be achieved through mental and physical exercises. Any method that offers increasing mastery over one's mental attitudes, belief systems, and behavior generally leads to an inner sense of well-being and joy. I share the view that such mental changes are possible to achieve in a variety of ways. In my discussion of mental imagery I point out how the mind can become the vehicle to carry you along a new path in life that will give you a renewed sense of self. Self-empowerment, an internal control over behavior, can lead to heightened aliveness and vitality. These are the ingredients that stir the mind to expand and at times reach transcendence or "flow."

Learning to control your diet and weight without becoming tied to special foods makes the process simpler and easier to follow long-term. Your changes will come about from changes in your thinking and subsequently in your behavior. You will discover, as you proceed, that your new mental attitude toward dieting can produce an increased sense of well-being that is accented by eating a normal healthy diet.

HIGH FAT DIETS

Most diets today do not prescribe levels of fat beyond the 30% recommended by the NIH or the ADA. Thus whenever a diet goes beyond these limits you should carefully consider the implications to your health. You should be wary of a diet that goes against all the known dietary facts that are associated with heart disease. Eating high levels of fats, especially saturated fats, increases the likelihood you will develop atherosclerosis, or fatty plague formation in the coronary and cerebral arteries, with its attendant heart disease and strokes. High fat levels are also implicated in various types of cancer and reduced longevity.

LOW FAT DIETS

Other diets stress a very low fat intake, relatively low protein, and high levels of complex carbohydrates. The most extreme of this group is the well-known Pritikin Diet, which was initially devised to treat heart disease. Weight loss followed the calorie restriction. Meats, eggs, and most types of fat are reduced or eliminated. Whole grains, fruits, and vegetables are emphasized. The revised Pritikin Diet allows a limited use of healthy fats that are high in omega-3 fatty acids.

Dr. Dean Ornish, who also advocates low fat diets, stresses the need of reducing fat intake to 20% in his Preventative Diet to protect against heart disease. In addition, he developed the concept of the Reversal Diet, which is essentially a vegetarian diet with a total fat intake of less than 10% and contains no saturated fat. The diet consists primarily of complex carbohydrates, namely whole grains, legumes, fruits, and vegetables. It is used by people with known heart disease and can reverse the effects of coronary atherosclerosis. The fact that atherosclerosis can be reversed through an extremely low fat intake suggests that a low fat diet would be instrumental in preventing or slowing plaque development.

OTHER DIETS

Other diets have been in vogue during the past half-century and many continue to creep back into the marketplace for a new generation of dieters. We have been regaled with the grapefruit diet that promoted a diet consisting of a grapefruit before each meal, very low protein, and restricted calories. The proponents of such a diet believed that the grapefruit contained an ingredient that accentuated the burning of fat and thereby caused you to lose weight. Such a diet worked primarily by water excretion and reduced calorie intake, and its subsequent weight loss was temporary for most people.

The New Cabbage Soup Diet, another quick weight-loss program that came with the warning to use only for seven days, also worked by water excretion and calorie reduction.

The New Beverly Hills Diet stressed a "conscious food combining" approach, using a single food per meal and severely limiting the diet to primarily eating fruits. The diet is very unbalanced and results in a very low and inadequate intake of protein and fat. During the brief diet period, usually 35 days, the dieter was essentially on a modified fast.

The Jenny Craig diet program uses a point system but does not restrict any kinds of food. The company also produces prepared foods that the dieter can purchase.

The well-known Scarsdale diet, another of the very low-carbohydrate, high-protein diets, also uses herbal appetite suppressants. There is no calorie counting and early rapid weight loss can occur. Such diets are low in fiber and other natural nutrients and can lead to constipation and nutritional deficiencies.

The Sugar Busters also espouse a low carbohydrate,

high protein diet believing, as in the Zone diet, that eating foods high in sugar elevates insulin and automatically causes weight gain.

Weight Watchers is a program that is found throughout the country. The calorie needs of each participant is determined and thereafter that person uses a prescribed program that provides a set number of calories daily. They sell prepared food that is generally nutritious and the group activities and support tend to be enjoyed. This is a safe program providing slow, healthy weight loss.

Other diet programs that combine calorie reduction with herbs or diet medications have come and gone over the years. Many dieters have tried a variety of programs designed to help them lose weight. Whether utilizing an extreme form of fat deprivation, or eating large quantities of protein, or reducing carbohydrates to a bare minimum, or using exotic foods or drugs, all the programs seem to work for brief periods of time for most people.

How can all these diets work, at least temporarily, despite being dramatically different from each other? Most of them work because they all advocate a decrease in calorie intake. On a short-term basis any reduction of calories will cause weight loss. In addition, certain diets may cause reactions that diminish one's appetite. For example, a very high protein and fat diet will produce an excess of blood ketones that frequently cause secondary symptoms such as nausea, headache, and a distaste for food, thus reducing one's appetite.

At times a diet with a carbohydrate intake of less than 10% of one's calorie needs can cause a more rapid breakdown of body fat for energy due to the lack of available glucose in the diet. The initial weight loss will be high. However, this is an extremely unhealthy diet due to the excessively high fat intake that accompanies very low carbohydrate diets.

The diet plans that tend to extend their benefits for many months and even years require that their users adhere strictly to the diet guidelines. Any cessation of the diet practice will result in a rapid increase of body fat and body weight. Thus, special foods, often provided by the author or backers of the diet program, are required. The devotion to the program becomes to some degree obsessive, often a necessary element to sustain allegiance to a particular diet. Maintaining a compulsive loyalty to such a diet often proves very difficult, if not impossible, for many dieters. Eating prescribed foods doesn't satisfy their continuing compulsion to binge and eat excessively.

OTHER FACTORS IN WEIGHT LOSS

These include the amount of exercise undertaken, water intake, use of diuretics or weight control pills, the degree of individual and group support, and the development of a dependent relationship with dietitians or weight loss programs.

Diets that advocate one type of food, usually carbohydrates like apples, oranges, or bananas, tend to cause, at least initially, a very rapid weight loss due to the rapid breakdown of fat deposits and to a lesser extent muscle tissue. This provides both energy and the amino acids and lipids for cell growth and cell replacement. Fasting and drinking only water causes similar weight loss.

Those who have reached their optimal body weight

often continue to use diets that deprive them of essential nutrients. Others maintain high levels of protein and fats that are potentially dangerous to their health. Although many of the low-carbohydrate diets advocate the avoidance of unhealthy saturated fats, they still tend to contain too much fat.

On the other hand, diets that are extremely low in fat are difficult to sustain and it is still not clear if such low fat diets increase life expectancy. The body needs certain fats for cell reproduction, which may be impaired with profound fat deprivation.

Regardless of the type of diet overweight people undertake, 90% to 95% of them will gain back what they lost within two years. Most regain their weight in less than one year. Dieters need to assess their potential for maintaining their weight loss. They should plan how to avoid regaining the weight as soon as they begin their diets.

Dieters should include stabilization periods as part of their diet program in order to maintain normal basal metabolic rates. Otherwise the syndrome of "I can't lose the last ten pounds" occurs followed by rapidly regaining lost weight as soon as normal eating resumes.

The population is growing heavier and heavier despite the vast numbers of diet programs available. It is estimated that 60% of the population of the United States is overweight and half that number can be considered obese. Over 500,000 people in the United States die each year from the complications of obesity.

The problem of yo-yo dieting must be addressed as a compulsive habit. To overcome this tendency to lose and then regain the weight requires a major change in your thinking. My program specifically deals with this fundamental problem in weight control and uses the mind-changing effects of mental imagery to combat this tendency. Through a series of imagery exercises, dieters learn to change those mindsets which have sabotaged their efforts at permanent weight control.

A truly effective weight loss program that doesn't deviate from known and accepted dietary practices gives you freedom from controlled diets. By using the five keys to permanent weight control you will be able to lose weight steadily while maintaining the pleasure of eating. And you will keep the weight off for the rest of your life.

CHAPTER SEVEN

Water

Among the five primary components that are the basis for this diet program, water serves a unique purpose. When used as described it will become a lifelong mainstay of your weight control program.

Filling the stomach causes the stretch receptors to send a signal to the brain that you have satisfied your hunger. The first primary control technique for both losing and maintaining weight loss is understanding that hunger is gradually reduced as the food and liquid that you put in your stomach increases. The more food and liquid in your stomach the less the hunger. This effect is independent of the calorie intake and has nothing to do with what constitutes a good diet. It has everything to do with the bulk that fills the stomach.

The stomach of the average overweight person requires approximately one quart or four full glasses of fluid to fill it. It may take less than three glasses in a person who is not overweight. Many very obese persons can drink six or more glasses of fluid before feeling filled. When water is drunk slowly without food it quickly leaves the stomach, which explains why some obese individuals can seemingly drink without cessation. Fluid drunk with food may remain in the stomach up to three hours during the first digestive phase.

If you put one pound of highly fat-laden food into your stomach rather than one pound of mixed vegetables, you would have consumed as much as ten or more times the calories of the vegetable mix. From your stomach's viewpoint one pound is one pound and the degree of hunger satisfaction is essentially the same. But the calorie difference in that pound can be enormous.

What does this mean in facilitating weight loss and weight control? The larger the quantity of food with the fewest calories the greater the weight loss and the more effective the control. Pound for pound, low calorie foods cause greater weight loss because you take in fewer calories to fill the stomach. Since most of you will be attempting to follow the recommended nutritional guidelines, vegetables, fruits, and grains will comprise a fairly large proportion of your diet. This will reduce the amount of fat-laden food that goes into your stomach. The greater the proportion of fruits and vegetables, the greater is the effect. Changing from a low to a moderately high carbohydrate diet will often result in a sufficient reduction of calories to satisfy much of your calorie reduction needs.

Knowing that adding bulk to your stomach contents will reduce hunger and thus reduce your food intake, you are now prepared to adapt water to your diet and weight control method. There's nothing particularly new about drinking water in a healthy diet. Most diets point out and even stress the value of water. What I emphasize is the amount and the way to use water.

Thus water will, in itself, help you control your food intake by filling your stomach with calorie-free liquid. The method of using water is quite specific and the degree of control it offers depends on how well you follow these directions.

Upon awakening, drink one or two eight-ounce glasses of water. At breakfast drink an additional glass of water just before you begin to eat. During your meal drink another glass of water. This is in addition to any juice, coffee or milk you drink. If you feel that this is an excessive amount of water, start your increased water intake slowly. The amounts noted above can be half as much initially.

At each additional meal you eat, whether just lunch and dinner or multiple small meals each day, drink one glass of water before you begin eating and at least one glass during the meal. Throughout the day whenever you feel like having a snack, no matter how small, always precede it with at least half a glass of water. Whenever you feel hungry or have an impulse to eat, try to limit the impulse to only drinking water and not eating the snack. Eventually you will be able to drink just water to satisfy your brief hunger pangs. This will enhance your control over the amount of food you eat.

You can drink water freely in your diet without concern. There is no evidence that drinking fluids of any kind with food interferes with digestion or absorption of nutrients. I have had hundreds of patients who have followed this diet and all have used water as described without any ill effects. Many foods are made up of as much as 90% water.

Other fluids can be drunk as desired. I have often been asked whether the water could be replaced with tea, coffee, soft drinks, or juices. Although these other drinks do provide part of your water needs, there are several reasons not to confuse them with the use of water for weight control. Some drinks have caffeine and this can influence your water excretion and your degree of thirst. Other drinks have calories to be considered. It's also easy to become dependent on drinks other than water. In general, use the water as suggested and the other drinks as part of your regular diet.

There is another benefit from drinking excess water. It helps prevent salt retention in the body. As you excrete this excess water through your kidneys some salt is excreted with it. Your homeostatic mechanisms will keep you from excreting too much water or too much salt. It's important to recognize that the excess water actually helps prevent fluid retention by reducing the salt level in the blood.

If you sense resistance to drinking this amount of water, try to evaluate why. I have often found that merely asking yourself questions about why you resist something is enough to overcome the resistance. The self-questioning implies you don't accept the resistance and inwardly that amounts to fighting it. Frequently, however, answering your questions will lead to a better understanding of your struggle to diet. Also your opposition is countered by your motivation to lose weight. It is very important to overcome any resistance to the use of water in the manner I described. In the chapter on the journal there is a section on resistance to various aspects of the diet, which includes the use of water. The journal will help you focus on the reasons for your resistance and help you overcome them.

Using water for diet control offers you an excellent

tool for both losing weight and weight maintenance. If you already drink this amount of water continue to do so but try to conform to the method I described. Your stomach doesn't care what fills it to reduce your hunger or craving for food. By using the water as described you will automatically decrease your food intake.

If you have any doubts about the effectiveness of water to reduce hunger I suggest you try this experiment next time you are hungry. Instead of eating any food, slowly drink water. At a certain point you will find you lose your appetite. It may take three to six glasses of water or even more for large people, but you will gain the understanding of the effectiveness of water for dieting. Many of my patients have told me that learning how to use water as a way of reducing hunger and controlling weight was the most important part of their weight control program. Water is also used in the special one-day diet that accompanies the use of the bathroom scale.

Due to other factors in hunger, such as blood sugar, insulin, a psychological need to feel something solid in your mouth, and relishing the taste of certain foods, hunger may return quickly. However, by mixing large amounts of water with food, it stays longer in the stomach as the food goes through its first digestive phase. Some of my patients moderately reduce their water intake after they have gained permanent weight control. At the slightest hint of any renewed impulse to overeat they immediately resume the full use of water.

If you are on diuretics, have a water retention problem, or find that large quantities of water cause bloating or indigestion, discuss this with your doctor.

If you find you are unduly thirsty and need to urinate frequently you should be examined for possible diabetes or other medical problems.

Drinking large amounts of water will increase your urinary output. However, it is a very important part of effective dietary control. For older people I suggest limiting the water intake after your last meal of the day to diminish the need to wake up at night to urinate.

CHAPTER EIGHT

The Scale

The innovative use of a bathroom scale addresses the negative feelings that most people have regarding weight gain. The scale should be considered a psychological assistant. Let's try a little experiment, one I do with all my patients who start the diet program. I want you to seriously reflect on what you feel and think whenever you step on a bathroom scale and see that you have gained weight. Take your time and really think about your reactions to the weight gain.

Most people feel guilty, disgusted, depressed, angry at themselves, or angry at the scale. Some people even kick the scale. Because of these feelings many overweight people never set foot on a scale, either when dieting or at any other time. They just don't want to know.

Not many feel elated, happy, or even mildly positive when they look at the number staring back at them and realize that they have gained weight. Many dietitians, knowing the negative feelings people have about gaining weight, advise their clients to use the scale sparingly or only when they come to the clinic or to a scheduled appointment.

What do these negative reactions do to the dieter? Negative reactions to gaining weight tend to accentuate one's sense of failure or loss of control. Although it may temporarily motivate some dieters to be more careful in what they eat or even to go on a more stringent diet for a day or two, it eventually increases the tendency to overeat. Eating satisfies a longing to feel good, to feel accepted, and to be loved. Eating, in a paradoxical way, reduces your sense of failure when you lose control and overeat. It is one of the reasons that losing weight is so hard to do.

When strong negative feelings grip a person there is a powerful urge to overcome them. To reduce guilt and self-condemnation a person will usually follow a path that has worked before. If eating had helped before, the inner belief system indicates it will work again.

So despite attempts to control eating, the power of this belief asserts itself and the dieter eats to restore a sense of well-being. The incident of the scale's telltale evidence of weight gain fades away and is replaced with the need to overcome guilt and anger. Over a period of time as the person realizes he's gaining more weight, the urgency to eat intensifies and his weight goes up and up.

If stepping on the scale increases guilt and anger the dieter will put the scale into a closet and avoid it. Thus the scale moves to the background of weight control. This part of the program is about to change that.

THE VOICE OF THE BATHROOM SCALE

It is necessary to change the negativism that you have

toward gaining weight. Weight control programs all have one thing in common. They try to help people lose weight by positive feedback when they have lost weight. In itself, this is a reasonable approach to dieting and should be maintained. Most diet programs do not reward the dieter when they have gained weight and thus the inevitable periods of regaining one or more pounds is met with self-criticism. My objective is to help you eliminate that negative feeling and convert it into a positive attitude.

Perhaps an analogy or two might help you to better understand this concept. If someone wanted to engage in stock speculation, one measure of his success would be how he reacted to the inevitable losses. The individual who examines and comes to understand the reasons for the loss and feels it was therefore a learning experience is more likely to become successful than one who becomes angry or depressed over every loss. In other words, the positive reaction to the unpleasant experience made the loss ultimately a positive experience.

Likewise, a student who gets angry at a teacher correcting her writing skills is much less likely to become a successful writer than one who sees the criticisms as beneficial and uses them constructively. For dieters, gaining weight is to be seen as a positive experience, for it will become a stimulus to improve their weight control using the special one-day extra water diet.

HOW TO USE THE SCALE

The scale will become your friend, your intimate companion on your path to weight control. Weigh yourself each day at the same time, under the same conditions, and wearing the same amount of clothes. The best time is in the morning just before breakfast and before eating or drinking anything. If you have lost weight or it is the same as the day before, acknowledge it with a smile. But if you have gained weight you are to feel *elated,* even if you have to initially force the feeling like an actor might.

Your reaction might go something like this. "Wonderful. I gained two pounds. I can't wait to lose it. What a great challenge. This gives me an opportunity to practice my special extra water diet." In other words the negative experience causes a positive reaction that initiates this special technique. The reason your positive reaction is effective is that it sets in motion a procedure that causes you to lose the entire weight gain by the following morning or the second morning at the latest. This is a key ingredient in your weight control plan that you will be able to use effectively all of your life.

THE SPECIAL ONE-DAY EXTRA WATER DIET

The event that sets in motion this special water diet is your discovery that you weigh more than you did the previous day. As you will be weighing yourself every day, those excess pounds won't accumulate over a long period of time. The weight gain may occur while you are dieting to lose weight or during periods of stabilization, which will be discussed shortly.

The steps to take are as follows

For one day only add three additional glasses of water to the water you already drink each day for every two pounds of weight gain. Some of my patients make certain they don't miscount their water intake by adding one additional glass of water before each meal. However, the time during which you drink the extra water doesn't matter.

During that same day decrease your calorie intake by 500 calories for each two pounds of weight you have gained. That is all you need to do. Even the decrease in calories doesn't have to be done. It would merely set you back one day in your diet if you decided not to further reduce your calorie intake the same day. By the next day you will have lost the weight you have gained because it was primarily water.

To gain an actual pound of weight in terms of muscle or fat you would have to have eaten 3,500 calories in addition to your normal calorie intake for each pound you gained. Thus, your two pounds of weight, if it were body flesh, would have required you to eat 7,000 additional calories in the previous 24 hours.

The probability of anyone eating that much extra food in one day while on a diet is remote. Rather, what happened was the excess food you ate included salt that was retained by your body. Due to the body's homeostatic mechanisms, the water retention needed to dilute the salt caused the temporary weight gain. Drinking the extra water eliminates that additional salt through excretion by the kidney, taking the extra water with it. Reducing your calories for one day takes care of whatever overeating you did the day before.

Some of my patients prefer to spread this additional 500-calorie reduction over several days and some prefer to ignore it entirely. It's up to you. What is essential is maintaining the discipline on a daily basis. If your control is not compromised by the minor dietary lapse the day before then there is no need to reduce your food intake by the 500 calories. However, if you find that you are gaining these extra pounds of water more than once or twice a week you should reduce your calories to avoid any accumulative weight gain. Also, carefully examine why you are beginning to overeat, and reestablish diet control.

In my experience, the special one-day water diet almost always works in one day. At times people on a diet are in a water retention period as the body is trying to accommodate to the lower body weight, and the technique doesn't appear to work. Don't get discouraged and don't do it more than two consecutive days, unless, of course, you overindulged the second day and thus added more water weight to your body. Just wait for the expected diuresis to occur. It will.

Why does this happen? Dieters who gain those two pounds generally have overeaten 500 to 600 calories the previous day. That amount of food will supply about 600 mg of salt over and above what their normal salt intake is. If your extra calories were higher or with a higher salt content you can easily gain four, five, or more pounds in one day. If by some chance you did not use the scale for several days and you overate, the weight gain can be higher. Don't despair. It is primarily water and will be excreted as you drink additional water during the day. If the weight gain came over several days then drink the additional water for several days. This process works.

Physiologically the kidney cannot excrete water without taking salt with it. The kidney will excrete the additional three glasses of water you drank as part of the special diet along with the added salt. The extra water that was retained because of the extra salt is no longer needed by the body and is also excreted. The total excretion generally occurs within 24 hours. In the same period, therefore, the weight gain of the previous day is eliminated. And your body's homeostasis will guarantee your weight will go back into equilibrium at the previous day's weight.

Now you can see why you feel positive when you get on the scale and see that you gained weight during the previous day. You now have the method of reducing your weight by a simple technique. There is no need for guilt or self-condemnation for there was no real weight gain. So bring that scale out of the closet and set it where it won't be missed. The scale is the first thing you will greet each morning. And it won't be long before you will indeed hail it as a friend.

BINGE EATING

What do you do if you go on a real binge and actually eat 7,000 extra calories of food in a single day? Anyone eating such huge quantities of food has a very different kind of weight problem than most overweight people. However, you would still do exactly what I described previously but must realize that the weight gain will not be overcome by the one-day technique. Also the amount of water retained by such a large amount of food will be in the neighborhood of 10 to 20 or more pounds depending on how much fluid was taken in during the binging.

In over 30 years of using this dietary approach I had only one patient whose weight at times fluctuated up to 20 pounds in a single day. Nevertheless, she followed the same technique and drank an enormous amount of water, which enabled her to lose those 20 pounds within two days. Her need to binge-eat required special mental imagery exercises and a period of psychotherapy before she could gain the necessary control to stop. It might be of interest to note that her type of overeating and weight gain (over 250 pounds) was the mirror image of anorexia nervosa. Instead of seeing herself as heavy the way a person with anorexia does, her body image distortion caused her to believe she was too thin.

In her childhood her father constantly urged her to eat, saying she was to thin for him to love. Like her obese mother who conformed to her husband's wishes, this little girl ate and ate to gain her father's elusive and withheld love. Other than at the dinner table where she could demonstrate how much she could eat, he rarely paid attention to her. Only by eating did she briefly gain her father's approval.

On days when you temporarily relapse and binge, make an effort to overcome any guilt by putting your energy into examining the reasons you ate too much. No one goes on a straight path to perfect weight control without some mishaps along the way. When you have your occasional relapses and regain some weight do not lose your resolve to continue your diet.

CHAPTER NINE

Exercise

Exercise helps you lose weight by increasing the amount of calories expended in a given time period. The calories burned during exercise vary considerably based on the kind of exercise, the length of time you exercise, and the degree of effort used.

In general, exercise can burn from 100 to as much as 400 calories per half hour. Although exercise is a very important part of dieting and weight control it is not an essential part of losing weight. After all, if you exercise and burn 500 calories but then eat an additional 500 calories, the exercise did nothing to contribute to weight loss. Weight control still boils down to eating no more calories than needed on a daily basis.

However, the advantages of making exercise a lifelong part of your daily activities are many. Any level of exercise improves general health. The benefit for your cardiovascular and pulmonary systems is well known. It helps control Type 2 diabetes, reduces high blood pressure, increases the immune system's ability to fight illness, diminishes the incidence of certain cancers, reduces tension and depression, and helps maintain a feeling of youthfulness.

Many dieters use exercise as an adjunct to losing weight. Exercise also tends to increase appetite. Thus, unless extra care is taken to control food intake when exercising it may not help in a weight loss program.

EXERCISE AND CALORIES

To give you an idea of some types of exercises and their range of calories burned, I've listed several activities and approximately what a 150-pound person will burn in a 30-minute period.

Sitting: 40 calories
Fast walking: 150 calories
Jogging: 350 calories
Running: 400 calories
Weight training: 250 calories

You can actually lose weight far more rapidly if you establish a daily calorie limit for your diet and maintain it on exercise days. Monitoring your weight is crucial, especially if you exercise vigorously or for prolonged periods of time. Increasing your water intake during exercise days will help you avoid eating extra food. Maintaining calorie reduction is easy if you use the scale daily. The scale will reveal any miscalculation on your part about the amount of food you are eating.

Another feature of exercise is the gradual replacement of fat with muscle. In a resting state muscle tissue burns up to twice the amount of calories that fat tissue burns. Therefore, building muscle bulk through exercise eventually becomes an important part of your permanent weight control program.

Exercise can help you diet and enhance your ability to manage your weight. On a diet you want to maintain muscle tissue and burn fat, which only occurs if your total caloric intake on exercise days is less than your total metabolic needs for that day. Fat is burned for energy and muscle is maintained intact by the exercise. Even during the diet period weight building exercises can add some muscle bulk. Aerobic exercises generally do not add as much muscle bulk as weight training exercises.

If you have arrived at your desired weight and continue to exercise while maintaining this weight, you will gradually change your body configuration as fat is burned and muscle is created. Muscle weighs more than fat by volume and thus your body volume will diminish while your weight remains the same. In this sense exercise is a component of weight control. At the very least, exercise can keep you from losing additional muscle tissue so common as we get older.

Exercise also benefits your cardiovascular system. Recent studies show as little as 30 minutes of moderately paced walking three or four times a week is beneficial to your heart. There appears to be no additional cardiovascular benefit from more prolonged and more vigorous exercise. However, there are other benefits, such as an improvement in your ability to engage in sports and more vigorous sex.

Exercise helps you retain the feeling of youthfulness and helps slow down the body's tendency to reduce the basal metabolic rate (BMR) as you age. The body continues to burn added calories after your exercise has ended. It also increases your feeling of well-being and vitality that adds to your motivation to keep your body weight constant. I encourage you to add exercise to your daily regimen if you have not already done so. Almost all diet programs advocate exercise as part of weight maintenance.

INCREASING YOUR BMR

Many people who have undertaken diets without a stabilization period have discovered at the end of their dieting that their metabolism has slowed down and they can no longer eat a reasonably normal meal. Often, they can raise their metabolic rate by a prolonged period of vigorous exercise.

During all exercise your metabolic rate is raised to burn stored sugars (glycogen) and fat to give you the energy needed for the physical activity. There is a tendency for the metabolic rate to remain elevated for up to 15 hours after exercising, especially when the exercise is strenuous. If you want to increase your metabolic rate, I suggest that you divide your exercise into two periods a day for up to six days a week and do aerobic exercises such as cycling, running, or swimming or use elliptical gliders, treadmills, or rowing machines. You might wish to add weight training to this routine. Prolonged repeated exercise maintains the heightened metabolic rate.

One to two hours of exercise a day for a period of several months is needed to make a permanent change in your BMR. A less arduous exercise routine over a longer period of time can accomplish the same change. Many of the dieters who followed this program for several months were able to increase their intake of food permanently. Generally I don't recommend starting such a vigorous exercise routine while on your diet program since it's difficult to assess the benefits while dieting. However, if you're motivated to add this to your overall plan for weight control, then by all means do so.

Many of my patients who used the enhanced exercise program also added certain specific mental imagery exercises, to be described later, to facilitate raising their BMR. Most reported that they had more energy, felt mentally and physically more alive, and were able to eat normally without gaining weight.

CHAPTER TEN

The Stabilization Period

Why do so many people who faithfully follow a diet and lose weight eventually gain it back? One of the reasons is that continuous weight loss over a long period of time almost always causes a decrease in the dieter's basal metabolic rate. The purpose of the stabilization period is to allow you to diet without changing your BMR.

Animal studies, as well as studies in humans, have shown that a calorie-restricted diet will initially cause a loss of weight. By maintaining the same calorie restriction the initial weight loss is rapid at first and then slows down. Finally, a dieter stops losing weight as a new level of body homeostasis develops. The calorie deprivation that caused the early weight loss is no longer looked on by the body as calorie restriction. The energy needs of the body are now met by the lowered food intake. Under extreme food deprivation the metabolic rate can be cut in half or more.

The new equilibrium allows the person to function with adequate physical stamina and a sense of well-being as though on a much higher caloric intake, providing the diet supplies the current metabolic demands of the body. If the diet continues to be restrictive and too much weight is lost, fatigue might be experienced during general activities.

In experiments with rats where the food intake was cut by up to 40%, the rats lost weight at first but eventually found equilibrium and functioned essentially normally. These rats tend to have a markedly increased life span on their continuing low caloric diet. Prisoners of war and people in concentration camps who were allotted extremely small daily food rations continued to live and function with only a fraction of the calories they previously had consumed.

THE CHANGING METABOLIC RATE

At the beginning of dieting each person has a set BMR. As the body takes in less food the regulatory mechanism that resides in the hypothalamus changes the caloric needs of the body. If your normal daily caloric needs are 2,000 calories and you reduce your calorie intake to 1,400 calories, the setting of the brain's metabolic thermostat will gradually change. It reduces the number of calories required for basal metabolic needs. Thus instead of continuing to benefit from the reduction of 600 calories and having the body burn an equivalent amount of fat to make up the difference, which is what causes us to lose weight, the amount of body fat burned gradually lessens. At some point in your extended dieting that 600-calorie reduction will produce no further weight loss. Your metabolic rate will have slowed to the point that you will be functioning on a 1,400-calorie diet. The length of time for this to occur depends on the consistency of the diet, the percentage of reduced calories, the amount of exercise you do, your initial weight, and probably certain genetic influences.

For the first month or so the changes in the metabolic rate tend to be minimal unless you are on an accelerated weight loss program. If weight loss is maintained at one or two pounds a week and not continued beyond one month, there is little discernible change in the BMR. However, if the dieting continues beyond a month there is a slowing of metabolism as the body adapts to the lower caloric input. Eventually you will lose less and less weight despite the strict adherence to the diet.

You probably know how hard it is to lose those last ten pounds. People who have been on previous diets often complain that they have to eat like a bird. They always have to be very careful of overeating. Otherwise, they immediately put on weight. The drastic lowering of the BMR sharply curtailed the body's ability to handle an occasional indulgence.

THE PRINCIPLE OF THE STABILIZATION PERIOD

A common failing of many diets is that they don't explain that once a person has lost the desired weight that he can't go back to eating the way he did before. The more weight a person has lost and the longer the time the diet continued the more likely that the metabolic rate has become fixed at a new low rate. A dieter's food intake is now limited by this lowered BMR.

Most people who have finally been able to attain their weight goal want to celebrate by again eating normally. To do so too quickly floods their body with excess calories and they begin to regain their lost weight. For many dieters their BMR may remain low indefinitely and for others months or years may elapse before such normal eating can begin.

To prevent the changes in basal metabolic needs I use a stabilization period for periodic weight adaptation. It should be used in all diets.

ONE-MONTH DIET, ONE-MONTH STABILIZATION

The optimal period of time to diet is one month. This should be followed by a stabilization period, also of one-month duration. During this period you will maintain your weight at whatever level it was at the end of your dieting month. I suggest that you always start each phase on the first of the month to simplify the scheduling of your dieting and stabilization periods.

By reducing your calories by 20% to 40% of your customary caloric intake you will lose one or two pounds per week. If you are steadfast in your calorie reduction you will lose four to eight pounds of body fat per month. In any diet there are periods when the body's homeostatic mechanisms will cause a retention of water to try to offset the weight loss. Thus the weight loss won't be steady.

During the first months of most diets there tends to be a rapid loss of body water as the kidneys excrete salt and water. Don't be misled and think that this is due to the burning of fat.

ADAPTATION DURING STABILIZATION PERIODS

Your weight on the last day of the month is to be maintained for the next month. You will learn as you implement the use of the stabilization period that it becomes a testing ground for you to learn to adapt to a new weight every other month. It is essential that you do not lose any more weight, or the purpose of the stabilization period is thwarted. Most dieters will find that within a few days they need to increase their food intake in order not to lose additional weight.

Each dieter must examine his feelings very closely during this period since it is hard to resist not continuing to diet month after month. But it is much better to face this struggle monthly and conquer any tendency to sabotage your diet than lose the benefit of the stabilization period. You will continue to use the scale and water and the special one-day extra-water diet if you find you have gained weight during the stabilization period.

Some of my patients questioned why I selected a month and not six or eight weeks or even two weeks for the diet and stabilization periods. In my experience one month seems to work for most. There is no doubt that the time when the decline in the metabolic rate begins varies in individuals. Differences in calorie restriction and how rapidly a person loses weight play a part. If a person loses weight very rapidly the metabolic rate declines more rapidly. This is one reason I suggest that weight loss be kept to no more than two pounds a week.

When you come to the end of your diet and have gone through a number of stabilization periods, albeit at lower and lower body weights, you will have become expert at regulating your food intake. Your final stabilization period continues for life and you should feel comfortable in maintaining weight control. Best of all you will be able to eat a normal diet. You won't suffer from the feeling of deprivation that occurs if your calorie intake is curtailed over a long period of time. And once you have gotten off the yo-yo cycle your BMR will slowly rise to accommodate your new level of activity.

Other Advantages

There are several other distinct advantages of the stabilization period. You need not be concerned about the amount of weight you lose during your dieting month. Even if you have not lost any weight during that period you must still adhere to the stabilization period concept. If you start a diet month at 150 pounds and you are still 150 pounds at the end of the month, you will stabilize at 150 pounds the following month. Often a person will say that since they didn't lose any weight their metabolic rate didn't change and they'd like to continue the diet instead of stabilizing.

There are two very significant reasons that adherence to the stabilization period is so important. First, during the month it is likely that there were fluctuations in weight due to brief periods of successful dieting followed by relapses. The BMR hypothalamic stabilizer was probably influenced by the gyrations and now needs a quiescent period. Second, you need to change your thinking about your weight, the food you eat, and what relapse means. During the stabilization period you will not have to be concerned about relapse but about keeping your weight constant. If you can't maintain constancy at a specific weight on a monthly basis it will prove harder to do it at the end of your dieting.

Your objective is to understand the causes of your

relapses through self-evaluation. You must move away from preoccupation about your weight and deal with your thinking and belief systems that govern your behavior. You are changing the way you think about your body, dieting, and weight control. You will be learning a new way of weight management that should be permanent.

During the periods of stabilization you will be adjusting to a new body size and a normal diet. You may believe you will have to double the length of your total dieting but in actuality your total diet time will change very little.

There will be no major change in your basal metabolic requirements so each period of dieting should be as effective as previous ones.

There is less likelihood of relapses, which tend to prolong the dieting period.

CHAPTER ELEVEN

Starting Your Program

Starting your program of weight control is more than beginning to cut down on your calorie intake. You must first establish a realistic mental picture of how you want to look. Make certain you evaluate anything that appears to be unrealistic in your body image.

THE DIET

There is no need for a special diet, a crash program, or diet medication. The focus is on factors other than food itself. The emphasis will be on improving your psychological health as well as your physical health. The framework to control your weight involves developing new belief systems that are related to how you eat, why you eat, when you eat, and what you eat. Such new beliefs will come from the practice of certain mental imagery techniques I shall outline later.

The program I am presenting is a new dietary approach that works for most overweight people. There are many possible diets for you. Eating food you enjoy and yet maintaining a healthy diet is the backbone of this program.

Since you will not gain weight if your calories do not exceed your daily needs no matter what combination of foods you eat, you could occasionally include some sweets and desserts in your diet. There is no need for specific foods in this program so you will eliminate the problem and expense of buying specially prepared foods that are a feature of some diet programs.

BEGINNING YOUR DIET

When you decide the time is right to begin your diet I suggest that you reduce your food intake by at least 20% of your normal caloric needs. Any reduction of calories will work. Cut back on your food intake moderately. There is no need to starve yourself and there is certainly no need to suffer while dieting.

It takes 3,500 calories to produce one pound of flesh. If you plan to reduce your calorie input by 500 calories a day you will lose one pound of actual body tissue, usually fat, per week. To lose 1½ pounds of body tissue per week you'll need to eat 750 fewer calories.

In most diets, and this one will be no different, more weight is lost in the early weeks of a diet as the body rids itself of excess salt and water. Eventually, it is only body tissue weight (primarily fat) that is lost.

By following the suggestions for the use of water, the bathroom scale, exercise, and the stabilization period, your diet program can begin. Utilizing mental imagery (see Chapter Twelve) to change your belief systems and behavior patterns completes the five keys to permanent weight control.

If you follow this program there will be no decrease in your metabolic rate. You will be able to lose the same amount of weight during your diet periods no matter how long you need to diet. The problem of how to lose those last ten pounds will not occur.

As a rule of thumb, it is easy to remember that protein and carbohydrates yield four calories per gram of food or about 110 calories per ounce. Fat yields nine calories per gram of food or about 250 calories per ounce. To maintain a steady weight the average person requires between 2,000 and 2,500 calories of food based on average activities. One's weight, degree of body fat, amount of exercise, age, degree of tension or anxiety, and certain genetic factors determine caloric needs.

In general the heavier a person is the more food is needed to maintain body weight. In a quiescent or rest state, muscle burns twice as many calories as fat. Thus body fat with little accompanying muscle would require fewer calories a day. The more muscle you have the more you can eat while in a quiescent state without gaining weight. For some very large and muscular men who spend several hours a day exercising in addition to having a physically active job it may take over 5,000 calories a day to fulfill their total metabolic needs.

The use of the scale makes the counting of calories relatively unimportant since your objective would be to either lose weight or keep your weight stable. You will be weighing yourself daily under prescribed conditions and using the special one-day water diet to regulate daily weight fluctuations.

CALORIE COUNTING

Even though you don't need to count calories, it is worth learning the approximate number of calories in various foods. This knowledge will become part of your internal regulatory mechanism. Most foods that you purchase in markets, excluding fresh fruits and vegetables, have the size of the helping and its calorie count on the package. After a while you will know your calorie intake when eating your favorite foods and it will act like a governor over your food input. A pound of tomatoes or lettuce or cheese or meat have markedly different effects on your feelings of hunger and the amount of food you will eat in a given period of time.

A few generalities about **fruits and vegetables** will make your calorie assessment of them relatively easy. On an ounce by ounce basis they tend to have fewer calories than other foods. The more the apparent water in them the fewer the calories. Therefore foods like watermelon, tomatoes, oranges, and leafy vegetables are very low in calories.

Vegetables range from about two to ten calories an ounce. A cup of spinach is about ten calories, one red pepper is 25 calories, broccoli is six calories an ounce.

Fruits range from about 50 to 100 calories per cup. Dried fruit is about 70 calories an ounce and fruit juices range from 80 to 120 calories for an eight-ounce glass.

Chicken breast and most fish vary from 35 to 50 calories an ounce. **Dark meats** and meat with skin or with fat laced through it are much higher.

Cheese is generally 80 to 120 calories an ounce.

Dry cereal is 80 to100 calories an ounce.

The calories in **alcoholic beverages** are determined by the amount of alcohol and sugar in them. There are

150 calories in a 12-ounce bottle of beer, 110 calories in a five-ounce glass of wine, and 160 calories in five ounces of sweet wine. One-and-a-half ounces of 80-proof liquor contains 100 calories.

Oils such as olive, corn, soybean, and canola are 125 calories per tablespoon. **Butter and salad dressings** range from 50 to 100 calories per tablespoon.

Most of us tend to eat the same foods each day and thus it becomes relatively easy to determine the calories. But again there is no need to do this to be successful. The use of the scale is an unfailing method of determining if you are eating too little or too much food on a daily basis.

HUNGER

Hunger develops from a variety of different elements that interact and determine when and how much food people eat. A hunger thermostat in the brain's hypothalamus sets in motion a biological rhythm that determines when it is time to eat. Blood sugar and the level of blood insulin contribute to this hunger need. The emptiness in the stomach produces feelings of hunger. Psychological conflicts can influence daily fluctuations in hunger. Depression, anxiety, feelings of loneliness, rejection, and loss can markedly change eating patterns.

We all tune into rhythms set by customs of eating at a particular time of day. The customary pattern of breakfast in the morning, lunch at midday, and dinner in the evening varies considerably. Different cultures regulate eating periods differently. Some cultures mandate dinner at 6 PM and others at 9 or 10 PM. The attendant population regulates their hunger accordingly. These rhythms are not fixed and can fluctuate in different circumstances.

Many individuals do not eat certain meals. Many skip breakfast despite the usual biological rhythms that would stir hunger in the morning. Others skip lunch. Some people eat small meals throughout the day. Eating habits are influenced by many things other than biology. Personal beliefs or mindsets help determine these differences.

Experiments to determine what influences these seemingly inherent bio-psychosocial rhythms have shown how flexible humankind can be. When people voluntarily entered a cave for an extended period of time without benefit of clocks or outside light they unknowingly changed many of their habit patterns. Under carefully controlled studies such people changed their sleeping and eating routines. The 24-hour cycle no longer determined many patterns that previously were taken for granted. Psychological needs, physiological stimuli, and group interactions affected their changes in habits, behavior, and time perception.

Hunger became regulated by personal reactions to blood sugar fluctuations, emptiness of their stomach, imagined or estimated time intervals, and various group interactions. It was surprising to find that some individuals reduced and even eliminated hunger pangs and conformed to a rhythm set by group adaptation.

Under conditions such as those described above, new rules develop out of necessity. Once a person accepts this new attitude or mindset his behavior changes. Eating patterns are thus changed by new beliefs.

The importance of these observations can't be

overestimated. By changing thinking or beliefs it is possible to change behavior. It thus becomes possible through mental exercises to reduce, eliminate, or radically change many habits we take for granted. This includes the feelings of hunger. And it can be done in a relatively short time.

In our everyday culture many people eat from one to six meals a day or more. Such people feel completely satisfied by their particular rhythm of eating. Those who eat one meal a day frequently combine it with multiple small snacks throughout the day. Some do not. Others only drink fluids and sometimes only water the remainder of the day. By using mind/body interactions we can modify our eating habits and overcome our essential physiological rhythms. Mental imagery and establishing new beliefs for dietary control are the keys to changing behavior.

CHANGING ATTITUDES AND BELIEF SYSTEMS

Every diet and weight control method requires a change in eating habits to work effectively. Such changes occur by modifying attitudes and beliefs. If you believe that the only way you can lose weight is by eating spinach and your desire to lose weight is sufficiently powerful you will eat only spinach. If you maintain motivation and continue your spinach diet you will eventually reach your desired weight.

The problem now arises on how to maintain weight stabilization. Certainly not by continuing to eat spinach. Despite your great resolve to maintain your weight, once the motivation to lose weight is over you need to resume normal eating. Unless during your weight loss period you managed to change your thinking about eating you're apt to resume your old eating pattern. And a short time later your weight is back to where you started. What is the message in this example? If you can actually lose weight on a specific type of diet, which requires a marked change in attitude and belief, then why can't you maintain it by changing other attitudes? You can. Let's examine the issue.

To understand how to change your attitudes and thinking about eating, first consider the underlying or subconscious cause of overeating. Where food is abundant eating has always been considered a very pleasurable experience. Eating tasty food, enjoying a good wine or other beverage, and indulging in a delectable dessert is part of the pleasure we seek in life. Yet such enjoyment of food is often equated with overindulgence in the diet-conscious person. Instead of delight in eating, the overindulgence causes feelings of guilt, depression, self-condemnation, decreased self-esteem, and a fear of again losing control over one's food intake. Such feelings occur in both the overweight person and those who have successfully lost weight.

Almost everyone who enjoys food is aware of the heightened pleasure that a good meal offers, especially when shared with friends and loved ones. Food is indeed an offering of closeness, sociability, equality, and friendship. These themes play out in feasts and eating indulgences. When these feelings are intense they become another powerful force that can contribute to overeating.

MASTERING WEIGHT CONTROL

For a weight control program to work, a way must be

found to help overcome these various psychological conflicts and barriers. Whatever the problem the dieter is struggling with, it needs to be faced and overcome. Otherwise changing attitudes for effective dieting will be difficult.

Weight control depends on eliminating the fear that you will be unable to follow any program and win the battle. You have to believe you won't lose control again. Also, in addition to the continuing weight control, you need to feel that you will regain the freedom to enjoy food and dining without guilt or other negative feelings.

It is possible to gain control over these emotions and finally find a way to lose weight permanently. By understanding the principles behind the five keys to permanent weight control, you will be able to use techniques to give you the confidence to lose weight, to control your weight and to enjoy eating again.

CHAPTER TWELVE

Introduction to Mental Imagery

The use of mental imagery to change thinking and behavior has been around for hundreds of years. Sometimes called visualization or waking dreams, mental imagery is used in hypnosis, behavioral therapy, meditation, yoga and plain ordinary daydreaming. Although actors, writers, and artists have used it for many decades, it has only recently become popular with professional athletes.

Actors use imagery to perfect their craft by visualizing their actions in movie scenes before they are actually filmed. Directors plan scenes and change props in their minds through imagery. Writers create new worlds and invent characters to fill those worlds through imagery.

Although the focus of this book is on helping you lose weight and develop permanent weight control, your knowledge of mental imagery can take you into other worlds of self-growth.

Many people use imagery to overcome illness. In 1978 O. Carl Simonton, M.D. wrote one of the first medical books, *Getting Well Again*, on the use of mental imagery to treat cancer. He discovered that terminally ill cancer patients who used prescribed imagery exercises in addition to their conventional treatment lived longer than a comparable group of patients being treated only by conventional means.

Not many years later Bernie Siegel, M.D. wrote his classic bestseller, *Love, Medicine & Miracles,* and explained how a person can "think" himself sick or well. His use of visualization techniques brought mental imagery into the homes of many people who sought new ways to foster good health as well as overcome sickness.

Today many more people have learned about mental imagery through outstanding teachers such as Deepak Chopra. We have learned that two famous musicians, Artur Rubinstein and Vladimir Horowitz resisted practicing the piano. Instead they would visualize playing entire concerts without physically moving a finger. Many read about the great power of mental imagery in the September 25, 2000 issue of Newsweek in the article "Olympic Mind Games." It reported how professional athletes spend hours visualizing specific actions and movements while sitting quietly in a chair with their eyes closed. Earl Woods taught his son, Tiger, to form a mental image of a golf ball dropping into a hole. The incredible putting skill of Tiger Woods is already legendary. Michael Jordan, Nancy Kerrigan, and Jack Nicklaus all practiced their moves mentally. Today most world-class athletes use mental imagery to maximize their performance.

To better understand how imagery influences behavior and mental attitudes let's enter the mind of a basketball player. To improve his shooting skills he would sit quietly and visualize himself standing some predetermined distance from a basket. In minute detail he would visualize his body posture, his arm movements, and the ball arching through the air on its way to the hoop. He would visualize making his movements perfectly. The player would practice mentally until he felt confident that his physical skill had been enhanced sufficiently for him to go and actually shoot baskets.

Athletes can develop and improve their skills almost as efficiently with imagery as with actual practice. However, to utilize the mental improvement of their skills the athlete must go out on a court or field and practice in real time and in real action what he developed through imagery. In addition, he must do daily exercises, practice team coordination skills, and maintain a healthy body to compete. No athlete would become great only using imagery.

CHANGING BELIEFS AND BEHAVIOR

By learning mental imagery techniques you will be able to change your behavior about eating and weight control. The exercises will help you develop a new set of beliefs about eating. You will learn that you can mentally control your food intake, your body size, and your emotional attitudes related to eating.

But like the basketball player and other athletes you must continue to do in reality what you are attempting to influence mentally. You have to continue your diet and the use of the four other parts of your program.

Visualization studies of Ian Robertson of Trinity College, Dublin, and Stephen Kosslyn of Harvard University show that visualization activates many of the same areas of the brain that actual physical activity does. When you imagine throwing a basketball into a hoop with deep concentration while sitting quietly in a chair, the same neuronal circuits and brain areas are affected as though you were engaged in the activity on a real basketball court.

PET (Positron Emission Topography) and MRI studies show mental imagery produces similar physical changes in the brain whether the activity is real or imagined. The effect is just as permanent with the imagery as with the actual activity.

Belief systems or mindsets involve mental attitudes that determine who we are, how we function as human beings, what we do, how we treat ourselves, how we treat others, and even how we treat the world we live in. Belief systems are positive, negative, or neutral.

Positive beliefs include having high self-esteem, loving yourself and others, and feeling that you are loved and admired. Other positive beliefs involve trusting yourself, knowing that you are creative and productive, and that you share your knowledge. Having the belief in your own integrity and ability to control your life is one that governs most other beliefs. If you believe you can achieve your goals, that positive belief will guide you toward them.

Negative beliefs are the opposite of the positive beliefs. If you believe you are incapable of attaining your goals the negative belief will thwart you. Other powerful negative beliefs that affect your ability to control eating include believing that you cannot consciously control your behavior and that an inner force or compulsion makes you eat. Believing that you cannot change your eating compulsion makes it difficult to remain motivated to continue your diet. Others such as a distorted body image, feeling unattractive and unlovable, and believing that only eating can fill your emptiness also interfere with dieting. A belief that you can never become thin is a major deterrent to dieting. It often makes people look at relapses as proof of this negative belief and results in their stopping dieting.

These negative beliefs often give rise to self-condemnation, guilt over excessive eating, depression, feelings of inferiority, self-hate, and feelings of emptiness.

An example of a strong negative belief that only some overeaters have but that all can understand involves the connection of food and love. If eating is your only way to feel loved, a compulsive eating habit leading to obesity may develop. Occasionally I'm asked why such a belief can't be considered positive. After all, if a person believes that food is equivalent to love and they feel filled and satisfied by eating isn't that a positive reaction to the belief? Although it may appear that way, this belief is really a substitute for real love. People suffer greatly when they use food as a substitute.

Some of my patients have cried when they tried to explain why they must eat. Without food they believed their life would be completely empty. Food was the only love they believed in. If they weren't able to eat to their heart's content they would be extremely unhappy. I have gently pointed out that their tears indicated the sadness they felt. They often responded, "I really want to be loved, but I know no one will ever love me. I can always rely on food." Food had become their love object and I understand how difficult it is to give up such love.

Neutral beliefs have little to do with conscious behavior but rather deal with unconscious or autonomous behavior. An example would be walking. We take for granted that we can walk. Situations or feelings do not generally influence it. But even the ability to walk can be changed. Under hypnosis a person can be made to believe that he can no longer move his legs and he can't walk. His inner belief has changed. Such behavioral change can also occur from fear. Being "rooted to the spot" or "paralyzed with fear" are common sayings that reveal our belief that our ability to walk can be changed. Other neutral beliefs, such as knowing we can chew food or use our hands to pick up food generally have no effect on compulsive eating. However, on rare occasions these automatic functions are compromised by emotional conflicts or a physical disease that will influence eating and would require appropriate treatment.

The power of beliefs

We all take for granted that we can't fly. But in dreams we become believers and easily fly. Sometimes in the awake state a delusion overcomes reality and a person believing he can fly may fling himself from a rooftop. Beliefs are powerful tools of the mind. They can operate for good or for bad. You are going to learn constructive beliefs.

Imagery is a powerful adjunct to your total commitment to losing weight and gaining permanent weight control. It is important that you do everything possible to change the negative beliefs that relate to your eating problems and cultivate a new group of positive beliefs. They will have much to do with your ability to develop a truly effective weight control program.

TYPES OF IMAGERY

We think of imagery as primarily visual. However, other sensory elements such as smell, taste, body movements, and sound may become part it. Imagery can be divided into four types.

Literal imagery

Images that are essentially like the object of the visualization. For example, a realistic looking mouth.

Symbolic Imagery

Images that are suggestive in appearance or action of the object considered for visualization. For example, a large open paper bag that represents a mouth.

Process Imagery

A series of literal or symbolic images that represent an activity, a changing procedure, or a continuous process. For example, visualizing the movement of food through the body starting with the mouth and ending in the colon. This would comprise a series of connected visualizations.

End State Imagery

Images that represent the final state of a desired process. For example, seeing yourself thin and attractive as the result of your dieting program.

CREATING YOUR IMAGERY PROGRAM

Overeating and becoming overweight has many causes. The imagery exercises and settings selected for this program are those I found to be clinically effective with many patients. Imagery settings are simply the visual description of the place or venue where the imagery will take place. For example, visualizing a dining room table filled with your favorite foods would be the imagery setting. The imagery exercise is what you do in that setting to help you overcome your compulsive eating. It can be as simple as waving your hand in a magical gesture and making the food disappear in a cloud of smoke. The imagery settings and exercises that follow cover most of the specific eating problems you have struggled to overcome.

Imagery to fit your personal eating problems

As each imagery exercise is described, try to imagine which ones will fit your specific eating and weight control difficulties. The imagery can be modified, changed, or combined. New ones can be added. Old ones can be eliminated. You may think of some others that will fit your needs. You will determine the continuing usefulness of whatever imagery you decide on. The use of imagery is a creative and dynamic way to modify thinking and behavior patterns if used with a strong belief in its effectiveness. It provides a time for your imagination to soar.

As you read through the various imagery settings and exercises try to determine which will become particularly useful in overcoming negative attitudes and compulsive behavior. It is quite possible that only one or two will be necessary. The effectiveness of this program is not dependent on the total number of different imagery exercises you undertake but rather on the appropriateness of the selections and how they are used.

Creating imagery to change beliefs

In examining the attitudes, feelings, and thoughts of patients for many years, I have concluded that the difficulty in maintaining weight control is directly related to a number of key negative beliefs. They include low self-esteem, doubting the ability to control one's life, and the feeling of being unattractive and unloved. Through effort and the persistent use of imagery, negative beliefs can be overcome and changed to positive beliefs. As you do the imagery exercises and maintain your diet these negative mental attitudes will gradually diminish and your self-esteem will improve. This improvement feeds on itself and becomes partly responsible for the success of these exercises.

The plan for creating your imagery program is simple and direct. First, you will choose the imagery setting that represents where your eating problem takes place. Next, you will decide on the imagery that will help you combat the specific problem presented in that setting.

The imagery helps create a new belief system to diminish or even eradicate this particular difficulty. For example, if your overeating is involved with a compulsive trip to the supermarket, the image of a supermarket would become the imagery setting. You would then mentally construct obstacles to entering the supermarket, such as surrounding the market with an electric fence that would shock you when you attempted to get past it. In this case, your new belief system states that the supermarket is no longer available to you for buying food for binge eating. The imagery does not interfere with your using the supermarket for normal food purchases. Your mind will always be aware that the imagery is being practiced for the specific purpose of overcoming harmful eating habits.

Practice this imagery exercise daily for weeks, months, or years as you continue your dieting and stabilization. Each exercise takes only ten to twenty seconds to do. Imbue it with as much feeling as possible. The imagery works because you want to change your eating habits. You want to make it work. You are opening your mind to your own suggestions because you want to lose weight. Imagery works because you have faith that your mind can control your behavior.

Deep relaxation induces a heightened degree of suggestibility to your own thoughts. Later, I shall describe a relaxation technique that I have used for many years in my practice.

As you read each imagery setting and its related imagery try to imagine how important each one is to your personal eating problem. From the beginning try to visualize each setting and each method that is described. Concentrate as fully as possible even though you are not yet using the imagery. Later when you determine what imagery will work best for you, your mind will have already become attuned to seeing imagery with vividness and deep feeling. These preparatory visualizations will help you develop highly intense, focused, and emotional imagery.

CHAPTER THIRTEEN

The Practice of Imagery

Imagery is best practiced in a state of deep relaxation. You can use any relaxation technique you wish, such as meditation, progressive relaxation, or deep breathing. The technique that I have used for many years is quick and effective and can be accomplished in the space of two deep breaths. It is important that you never practice this technique while driving a car.

THE RAG DOLL TECHNIQUE

Sit in a comfortable chair. Relax your body. Close your eyes. Visualize yourself as a rag doll. To enhance this visual picture it may help to shake your arms and legs a few moments in a loose manner like a rag doll.

Take a slow, deep breath. As you slowly exhale pour your mental self into your rag doll self. Take another slow, deep breath and again slowly exhale and once more pour your mental self into your rag doll self. You should now be in a deep state of relaxation.

Repeat the rag doll relaxation technique a few times until you are comfortable with it and can truly feel the deep relaxation that is conducive to practicing the imagery exercises.

For those who desire to gauge the timing of your breathing, count to four on inhaling, hold your breath to the count of two and then exhale to the count of four. As soon as you feel comfortable with the rate of your breathing there is no need to count.

STARTING YOUR IMAGERY

To start your program, determine which of the imagery exercises appeal to you. I suggest that you start with one or two exercises plus the end-state imagery. Most dieters experiment extensively in the first few weeks of developing their imagery. Rarely do the first imagery settings remain constant throughout their dieting program. Even when the initial imagery fits the problem, it's apt to be modified as your experience with imagery grows. Above all, try to be as creative as possible and enjoy developing it. Within a week or two you will have created a useful program that fits your particular needs. These exercises will become an important part of your permanent weight control.

The end-state imagery should be how you want to look and feel at the end of your dieting. Your emotional state should include high self-esteem, exuberance, and joy in your new sense of well-being. Even if you are beginning this diet program in a state of depression or self-doubt, rise above those feelings when you do the imagery.

In doing the end-state imagery you must believe that you will reach your goal. The belief is what feeds your auto-suggestibility and changes your thinking. Even if you have trouble fully believing the power of imagery at first, make believe that you do.

Timing and Frequency

Try to do the full program a minimum of three times a day and, if possible, as much as 20 times a day. Frequently, ten to twenty seconds per exercise is sufficient. Thus a program with five to ten different exercises may only take a few minutes. Experiment with doing the exercises for longer periods of time alternating with shorter periods but with greater frequency until you determine what feels best. Trust your judgment. Practice and experiment until you find that combination of exercises and time that works for you. Gradually the benefits of these exercises will become increasingly evident. You will experience a change in your mental attitudes about eating and your ability to control your weight.

The heart of this or any other diet program lies in your belief in its effectiveness. Losing weight is the easy part. Many programs offer effective techniques to lose weight. But determining whether you have achieved permanent weight control can't be known until time has passed. So much depends on your motivation and resolve to continue the program. Ultimately it's your belief in yourself and in your sense of empowerment that will give you control over your eating.

CHAPTER FOURTEEN

Imagery Settings and Exercises

You are attempting to change a deeply ingrained belief system that has governed your life for years. Under appropriate influences your mind can change almost anything. Persistence, continual motivation, and a strong belief in the process are required. The negative conditioning that influenced your eating compulsion requires powerful imagery to counteract. The imagery described offers you that power.

All the examples of imagery in this book can be modified in any way you desire. Identify the nature of your compulsion and create a series of imagery settings that fit your needs. The ones I use, which come from the experiences of many of my patients, are suitable for most dieters. The mind doesn't care what imagery is used provided it satisfies your belief that it is fighting your eating compulsion.

Most of the examples are in the category of symbolic imagery. The imagery is merely creating new thoughts and ideas that eventually become a belief, a new mindset that says the food in the refrigerator, cupboard, or on a table is not for overeating or binging. Have no fear that this will keep you from normal use of these places. Your mind will always know your intent. That is true for all the imagery I describe.

None of my patients have ever told me that the imagery exercises interfered with their normal enjoyment of food. Actually, they enjoyed eating even more once they gained control over their weight. The imagery diminished or eliminated their conflicts associated with food.

Some of the following settings and exercises may not apply to you personally. Nevertheless, try to visualize all of them to help develop your facility in creating imagery. Some of my patients found it difficult to use negative imagery and preferred to use only positive imagery. Each person must decide what is useful for him or her. Experiment with different kinds of imagery. Create an imagery program that works for you.

THE HOME

Any place in your home where food is present or where you overeat can be the imagery setting. The food can be visualized in the refrigerator, on the dining table, in cupboards, on coffee tables, at work areas, or on your bed. Exaggerate everything and be free with your feelings. As you create your imagery, write them in your journal.

End each exercise with the positive statement that you will no longer binge or overeat.

The refrigerator

- A heavy iron chain encloses the refrigerator and makes it impossible to open. You tell yourself that the refrigerator is no longer available to you for excessive eating.

- The door is cemented close.
- A guard dog threatens you when you attempt to open the door.
- A thick, transparent, and impenetrable wall stands between you and the refrigerator. You can look at it but you know you cannot touch the refrigerator door.

Case illustrations

One of my patients who only binged by raiding the refrigerator visualized opening the refrigerator door only to find another door. She opened the second door, then a third door and continued to open as many as 200 doors. After doing this exercise for several weeks, she began her actual diet. Her imagery was accentuated by the intense feelings she put into her imaginary actions. She made each successive door heavier and heavier as she opened one after another. She told me that when she had become mentally and physically exhausted, she knew that overeating was just too much work. So she stopped.

This is a good example of a change in a belief system. The food in the refrigerator no longer supplied the satisfaction it once did. She continued the same imagery during the months it took her to lose weight. She followed the program scrupulously, never skipping a stabilization period, solidifying her determination to permanently control her weight. She knew she would never overeat again. And she was true to her word. She lost over 60 pounds in 15 months.

I generally don't advise using parental figures to prevent your opening the refrigerator since it is better to put up obstacles that are not based on parental criticism, judgments, or control. However, a patient of mine used such imagery effectively.

She imagined her mother and father guarding the refrigerator to keep her from "stealing" food. They called her names and threatened to beat her. In the imagery she screamed back and saw herself growing taller and stronger. They finally fled to avoid her anger. It wasn't until she had defeated them that the refrigerator door was free to be opened.

With a cry of power and relief she hurriedly opened the door only to find a grinning, hands-clapping child sitting inside the refrigerator. No food. Just the child. The child was herself at the age of five. And as she stood there staring, the child flung herself out of the refrigerator and buried herself in her arms. Both the child and the adult woman cried together. By having overcome the dominance of her parents she felt that she no longer needed to overeat.

This imagery, which was repeated for many months, fit a particular person whose overeating was tied to a personal conflict in her past. When she was a small child her parents dreamed of her becoming a world-class athlete. They stressed food control as early as the age of three, making the child feel guilty over any indulgence in eating.

The conflict resurfaced when the woman had her first child. She said that she was "horrified" as she watched herself repeating the actions of her own mother. Instead, with great effort, she deliberately controlled her tendency to restrict her daughter's eating. But guilt over defying her mother's strictness about eating, which had remained subconscious all those years, played out through her own compulsive overeating. She hated herself for becoming obese. The resolution of her eating difficulty was not easy and she needed a number of other imagery settings to facilitate her control. Almost all of her imagery during three years of psychotherapy and dieting came from her own imagination.

Her visits to me were only monthly and in the final year I saw her only twice. At the end of three years she had lost almost 100 pounds and gained an entirely new way to live and feel.

Other barriers to the refrigerator

In this group of imagery settings you can create internal obstacles to prevent using the food in the refrigerator to binge or overeat. In each case, first imagine opening the refrigerator door.

- You find the refrigerator completely empty.
- You find that all the food inside is spoiled and inedible. A strong odor of decay emanates from the food You gaze at the food in disgust. You swear that you will never go near the refrigerator for binging or overeating again.
- A terrifying animal is inside guarding the food. As you reach for the food the animal attacks you. You are terrified. You know that you will not use the refrigerator again for binging

From this series of imagery settings you can see that there are differences in the level of emotion you may want to introduce into your own imagery. Some overeaters prefer a milder form of imagery and some prefer extreme degrees of horror. Whatever imagery you use, always visualize the scene with exaggerated emotions and end by saying with great conviction, "I'll never binge on food from the refrigerator again!"

Table food

Although you will be presented with a few examples of imagery exercises, there is almost no limit to how they can be visualized. The settings are generally the same, namely seeing your favorite foods or an abundance of any foods on a table that you use at home. Remember to use your imagination freely in the following imagery exercises.

- You sweep all the food off the table with a flourish of your arm and watch the food scatter far and wide.
- You overturn the table with extreme anger at the fact that the food on the table is trying to tempt you. You see it splattered all over the floor.
- As you reach for the food you see it turn into something repulsive and completely inedible.

Some patients have imagined blowing up the table with dynamite. Others have seen themselves with high-powered fire hoses washing the food away. A few have waved their arms, said a magical incantation, and watched the food disappear. It makes no difference what symbolic or literal imagery is used. Your mind knows your intent.

End the above imagery exercises with some variation of the following. *I will never take food off any table again for overeating or binging.* Say it with fervor and absolute belief.

A cupboard filled with food

If you tend to use the cupboard as your source of food for binging or overeating use similar imagery that you used for raiding the refrigerator. As you develop greater facility using imagery you will enjoy using your imagination to create wild and unique images. You can't overdo the use of imagery in whatever you are trying to change in yourself. Certainly with dieting and weight control the more the merrier. Engorge yourself with images instead of food.

By now you may be smiling at the utter simplicity of the imagery. Some of it is quite funny to imagine and it doesn't hurt to have fun doing these exercises. Also, the mind doesn't care how simple or in what form you make the images. As you construct imagery to overcome your compulsion to overeat, you are using the power of your mind and your strong desire to control your food intake. Your personal imagery will become the basis for your new beliefs and help you develop a lifelong weight control program.

OUTSIDE THE HOME

We eat out at restaurants, in the homes of friends, at bars, in hotel rooms, from street vendors, in automobiles, in airplanes, and on cruise ships. We eat full meals or just snacks. Most overeaters eat excessively outside their homes at times. Some only overeat away from home, just as some only overeat in the confines of their home. If you tend to overeat outside your home, think where you do it and create the imagery to fight against those particular sites. Be as imaginative as you can.and believe that it is changing your beliefs about eating.

The following are examples of imagery to be used outside the home.

- You imagine yourself screaming at someone who offers you food. You can holler "NO" or "STOP IT" or you can tell them to leave you alone. You will never accept food from anyone again.
- You see yourself hitting away the hand of the person offering you the food. Do it with anger and force as though it's an insult.
- You visualize knocking the tray of food into the air.
- You turn the offered food into something noxious, frightening, or vile.
- You smash your own fingers with a hammer as you reach for food.
- You imagine a waiter in a restaurant refusing to serve you. He could scream that you are a pig and they don't serve pigs in the restaurant.

One patient who used to overindulge in restaurants created imagery where the waiter would come over and pour water on her head or stuff a towel in her mouth or have two men in white coats enter the restaurant and carry her off if she dared to ask for food.

Case illustration

A patient imagined the food attacking him. He visualized a piece of meat he was trying to eat with an enormous mouth filled with pointed teeth that reared up and bit him. He imagined a piece of fish sticking fishhooks in him. Vegetables would suddenly swell up and try to swallow him. A watermelon with an outboard motor would drive into his mouth and down into his stomach where it exploded spewing watermelon seeds in all directions. This patient had so much fun trying to figure out all the ways different foods could assault him for overeating that he became a believer in weight control through imagery.

Long after he had gained control over his weight he continued to conjure up new ways of being assaulted by different kinds of food. This man also used end-state imagery daily as his way of changing his negative belief about his body. He lost over a hundred pounds using this diet and weight-control technique.

To reiterate, all imagery exercises should end with an affirmation that you will never overeat again or with some imaginative variation of this statement.

FOOD MARKETS

Grocery stores supply most of our daily food. Since it is the normal way to purchase food you need to distinguish between normal food for you and your family and food bought for binging. For binge eaters any food can be used, so the distinction is only partial. The imagery we're concerned with now is going to the market to buy food for overeating. Even if you include such food purchases with your normal food needs, this imagery can still be used. Your mind always knows your intent.

Again, let your imagination run wild. The imagery can be anything that prevents you from entering the market or stops you from leaving the market with food. It could be something that foils your attempts to obtain food while in the store. Your imagery should primarily address how you use the market for overeating.

If you plan going to the market to buy food for binging, your imagery should involve the entrance to the market. If sudden impulses to binge are stimulated by being in the market, address that area. If entering the store, being inside, and leaving the market, all contribute to your binging create imagery in the three areas.

Imagery for entering the market

- An outside guard refuses you admittance to the grocery store. This can also be a vicious guard dog or a dragon spewing out fire or a platoon of police with drawn guns.
- The grounds are flooded with oil and you continually slip as you attempt to approach the market door.
- The store explodes as you approach it.

Case illustration

One of my patients imagined a 20-foot-tall giant standing by with a lasso whenever he tried entering the market. As soon as he approached the door the lasso would come whirling out of the air and envelop him, then drag him high into the air. The patient who was afraid of heights was terrified. When asked to describe the man with the lasso, he said it was a giant version of himself. Psychologically, this image was very constructive since it made this patient believe more fully in his desire to stop his overeating.

Imagery when you are inside the market

- A person walks next to you and removes all unnecessary or binge type food that you put into your food cart.
- As you approach food to place into your cart it changes into something terrifying or inedible.
- The interior of the store gets flooded and all the food is under water.
- A fire erupts and destroys the food that you want.
- The food blows up in your face.

Make the food funny. Humor is sometimes a very effective imagery tool to help you avoid food. You can reach for a box of chocolate cookies and see the cookies jump out of the box. The cookies could have faces and stick their tongues out at you or laugh or scream at you. Food can float into the air just out of reach with you frantically trying to grab it. You can either react with uncontrollable laughter or with total frustration. Either way, know that you would never eat such food again.

Imagery as you exit the market

- The door is locked and you are trapped. You will never be able to leave with your food.

- Guards similar to those who tried to prevent you from entering the market are standing there looking for overeaters.
- As you begin to exit the store with forbidden food a very loud alarm bell rings and people run toward you screaming "Thief." Police quickly put you in handcuffs and make you lie on the floor. They yell and stomp on you.

Normally you create one imagery exercise for each type of overeating situation. However, some circumstances are so important in your overeating scenario that several exercises are required to combat it.

One patient created a series of images for her venture to the market. She never overate unless she first went to the store to buy food for binging. Whatever she bought on that trip was consumed in a frantic binging episode. It was crucial for her to stop this compulsive habit in order to control her eating.

Case illustration

This patient created imagery that included a number of obstacles to keep her from entering the market and, in case she managed to get inside, to prevent her from leaving it.

We used process imagery in her case. We set up several different obstacles to prevent her from entering the market, each one more difficult than the preceding one. So even if she managed to get by the final obstacle and entered the market, she would be beaten, tarred, and feathered. Her hair would be cut off and her face smeared with filth. Finally, an enormous, heavy ball and chain would be tied to both feet making walking very difficult.

This patient practiced her imagery 20 times a day and each time it would change. Sometimes she would manage to get into the store, other times she was stymied by the obstacles. Either way she was developing a new set of beliefs that indicated that going to the market to buy binge food was devastatingly punitive. The market was slowly becoming taboo. She was losing the compulsive urge to buy food for binging.

The difficulties of entering the market exhausted her. But her real undoing was trying to leave the market. Again a series of increasingly difficult obstacles were placed at the exit. Some of her imagery was deeply distressing but she was determined to end her compulsive use of the market for buying binge food.

In her imagery her obstacles included being made to strip so her entire body could be searched for hidden food. Cameras recorded everything that happened to her including showing her obese body covered with dirt. The cameras deliberately distorted her body. She told me no witch was ever as repulsive as she was.

Finally, she visualized that despite the terrible obstacles, she persisted in her efforts to exit the market. As she made one last attempt, an enormous man dressed in a flowing white gown suddenly appeared and proclaimed that she must never come into the market to buy food to binge again. He told her that she would now rise above her desire to gorge on food and know that she has now been redeemed from her horrors of overeating. The balls and chains fall from her body.

She said her imagery ended with a profound feeling that she had gained the power to stop binging.

This patient was only 37 years old when she first came to see me and she could hardly move or breathe due to her obesity. At 5' 1" she weighed over 250 pounds and had become suicidal in her shame and disgust with herself. Of all of the overweight patients I've worked with she was among the most lost and depressed by her condition. But she was also one of the most motivated to overcome her lifelong obesity. She had reached the end of the line. Nothing had ever worked for her. Her previous diets were torture. She felt that no one wanted to come near her.

After the first four or five weekly visits during which she created the kind of imagery that would work for her, I saw her monthly. Each imagery experience took five to ten minutes. They were like movies in her head and constantly changed as she sought ways to make them more and more grotesque. She practiced the imagery 20 times a day, as I had instructed her. On some days it went as high as 50 times. She was determined to lose weight.

She drank enormous quantities of water. At times I became alarmed at the amount she drank each day. But she assured me that for the first time in her life she governed her existence with a will to live and she knew how much water she needed. Despite my cautioning her against it, many of her diet days were essentially fasting. As determined as she was to lose weight she was equally determined to keep her weight constant during the stabilization period. And she was true to her resolve.

After losing over 50 pounds the first year, she cut back on the frequency of her imagery but not on the ferociousness. A beautiful and tender person was finally revealed as she began to accept herself. She cried when she described the cruelty of children who ridiculed her during her childhood. I wept with her as she forgave those children who had caused so much suffering but "didn't know what they were doing."

In addition to controlling her eating she used the imagery to develop a hidden artistic talent. When I last saw her she weighed just 152 pounds and was exercising regularly. She was truly enjoying her life and her new sense of self. I received one card from her about eight months later telling me that she weighed 125 pounds and had complete control over her compulsive eating. She continued, she said, to do the same kind of imagery once or twice a day and was hoping to lose another 15 to 20 pounds before stopping her diet.

Stories of very heavy people losing enormous amounts of weight are not uncommon. Physicians involved with diet and weight control have had many in their practice, as I have. My emphasis is not only on helping patients lose weight but on showing them how to change their thinking and gain power over their compulsive behavior.

Even with the use of the five components of the diet program there is no guarantee that everyone will find the motivation and persistence to establish the control they desire. It takes time and consistency and it is not always easy, but the effort will prove fruitful. The rewards will be yours for life.

THE MIND-BODY CONNECTION

We are now going to develop imagery exercises that involve biological and physiological mechanisms.

Using imagery it is possible to change your pulse rate, increase your body heat, and influence other bio-physiological systems. For example, to change your pulse rate using imagery you can try the following exercise. You will need to practice it consistently over a period of time to obtain results. Imagine your body immersed in hot water and becoming overheated. Your pulse will rise in an effort to reduce the body heat even though this is happening in your mind.

You may have seen news broadcasts of monks in the Himalayan Mountains wearing only a loincloth, sitting in the snow at temperatures well below zero. Strictly by mind control they caused the snow to melt around their body. These monks practice Yoga and mental discipline many years to gain that degree of control over bio-physiological aspects of their body.

Imagery can make certain skin diseases disappear and headaches vanish. It can even slow down the growth of cancer cells. Although we are not certain how the mind affects the body, the fact that it does is well established. The mind-body connection is now accepted in most branches of medicine.

You may feel that you gain weight without overeating and that some problem in your digestive system is at fault. We already know that continuous dieting can reduce your metabolic needs. Could other digestive changes have arisen in periods of your yo-yo dieting? There is no clear-cut answer to this question but there is nothing to lose by incorporating digestive system imagery into your daily exercises.

You have already constructed imagery to reduce the amount of food you eat. Now through process imagery you can attempt to modify how food is digested and absorbed once it is eaten. You will work toward gaining a new belief system that the food you eat will not be digested and thus will not enter your body to become fat. Using process imagery you will attempt to modify the digestion of food starting with the mouth and continuing through the esophagus, stomach, small intestine, and colon.

You must create this imagery with complete conviction that you have the ability to change your digestive processes. Try not to question the validity of this process even though you may not understand how it works. In the same way that a person can change his heart rate or his temperature through imagery, he can modify his digestive processes. It is by autosuggestion that imagery works on the mind and body. It is part of the development of your new belief system.

THE DIGESTIVE SYSTEM

We will divide the digestive system into its component parts starting with the mouth and ending with the colon. Once we have clearly established imagery for each component of the system we shall combine them into a fluid series of images that carries the food through all parts of your digestive system. Your development of process imagery should feel natural and acceptable to you. Modify it until it does.

Imagery for the mouth

To prevent putting food into your mouth, use imagery that fits your method of eating. Do you stuff your mouth? Do you swallow food with minimal chewing? Are you a nibbler who never stops eating? Do you just eat too much? No matter what your eating style is, the following imagery can help erect mental barriers to overeating.

- Imagine putting adhesive tape over your mouth as you approach food. You are thinking *I'm not going to eat. I'm not hungry. I don't want to eat. I'll never overeat again.*
- See yourself putting food into your mouth and immediately spitting it out. Exaggerate. The food can travel long distances or explode when it hits something.
- Your mouth begs for food and you stuff it with a towel which also makes you gasp for breath. You can yell at your mouth as though it's an independent organ, *that's what you deserve for being so greedy and for never knowing when to stop eating.*
- Your mouth screams at you for feeding it poison. You can admonish it by saying, "all unnecessary food is poison."
- No matter how much food you stuff into your mouth it refuses to chew it. In this case your mouth is determined to take a separate stand as though you don't have the will to stop overeating. Your mouth has become your ally in your fight to control your food intake.
- Imagine there is no saliva being produced that normally aids digestion. If you decide to use this imagery, then stopping all digestive juices throughout the digestive tract should follow it. You would then visualize all food you ingest

traveling through your system without being absorbed.

Imagery for the esophagus and stomach

The possibilities of imagery for these two organs are endless. Try to use experiences you have had with eating that have proven uncomfortable or even painful and disgusting. For example, do you feel bloated after eating, or have a burning sensation in your abdomen, or throw up, or belch? Perhaps you have abdominal pain during or after eating. These symptoms frequently are connected to conflicts the eater has with his food. If you incorporate them into your imagery be clear in your mind that you are now connecting the symptoms to overeating. If the symptoms have been persistent, I advise you to have a medical evaluation by your physician before starting your diet program.

Remember that you are attempting to thwart the body's wish to break down, digest, and absorb the food you have eaten. If you can somehow trick the body into diminishing your digestion of food by even a small percentage it will assist you in your diet program.

You can use either literal or symbolic gastrointestinal imagery for the individual exercises. If you know and can visualize the actual body organs you can use literal imagery. It doesn't have to be exact. Otherwise stick to symbolic. For example, an esophagus can appear as a narrow tube of muscle and connecting fiber tissue or you can visualize it as a straight rubber tube.

- Imagine tying a string around the upper or lower part of your esophagus. Any food that managed to get past the mouth is stopped here.

- Create a series of tubes connected to your esophagus that takes the food directly to the colon without being digested.

One patient imagined a furnace in her stomach that burned all the food she ate and thus could not enter her body as fat. When she began to lose weight using this imagery we analyzed how it occurred. What we found was she ate more slowly because she would patiently wait for each mouthful of food to be thoroughly burned in her stomach. She did this consciously knowing it would reduce the amount of food she ate. Even after she reached her weight goal she continued to use the imagery before each meal and at least several other times day. She told me she never wants to forget that it is her mind that caused the change. The continuing use of the imagery is her daily reminder of that fact.

Imagery of the small intestine

Digestion and the absorption of nutrients primarily take place in the small intestine. This follows the partial digestion from enzymes in saliva and gastric juices. Enzymes produced by tiny glands in the mucosa (lining) of the small intestine plus a variety of enzymes from the pancreas and liver finish the breakdown of proteins, fats, and carbohydrates.

Bile from the liver is added to the other enzymes and acts like a detergent to break down the fat. Large molecules of food enter the small intestine where they are broken into small molecules capable of being absorbed into the bloodstream. They are carried to various cells for use or storage. Some go to the liver for further breakdown and utilization. Whereas food remains in the stomach for up to three hours slowly being broken down by gastric juices, its journey through the small intestines can be measured in minutes.

We create imagery for the small intestine to prevent absorption of the small molecules of food. Unlike imagery for reducing binging and overeating that can be observed, there is no way we can see how and if this imagery works. But since we know we can influence bio-physiological reactions, imagery may influence this final phase of digestion.

The imagery exercises I'm suggesting are some that patients have used. However, none of my patients used process imagery for the digestive system as their only imagery exercises. It should be used only as an adjunct to the other imagery exercises.

- Visualize partially digested food moving through the 30 feet of the small intestine in seconds. It moves so rapidly nothing can be further broken down or absorbed.
- Imagine plastic sheeting covering the entire lining of the small intestine preventing any intestinal juices or enzymes, including those from the liver and pancreas, from being secreted into the intestine. The food passes through without any digestion or absorption.
- Visualize thousands of tiny glands in the intestinal wall suddenly drying up or refusing to secrete enzymes into the intestine.

Imagery of the colon

By the time the remaining food reaches the colon most of the digestion and food absorbed for energy is over and the colon reduces the water content and prepares the remaining food for elimination. Intestinal bacteria help break down the residual food and are excreted with the fecal matter. However, there are many dieters who believe that chronic constipation adds to their difficulty in losing weight. If you have such a problem you can add imagery to overcome the constipation and bowel stagnation.

- Imagine large amounts of undigested food entering the colon where it is quickly eliminated.
- Imagine the colon having vigorous contractions that quickly expel the stools.
- Imagine a roto-rooter cleaning out your colon as it would a blocked drain.
- Imagine the stools as being soft and able to be easily expelled.

End-state imagery for the digestive system

If you don't feel a need to change the digestive system, yet want to include imagery that could eradicate minor problems, I suggest the use of end-state imagery. It is used to show a state of being that is free of illness or problems.

- Visualize the entire process of digestion by seeing food go into the mouth, down the esophagus, into the stomach, into the small intestine, and finally into the colon without any sign of illness or constipation.

- Visualize the digestive tract and its inner lining as gleaming white and in pristine health.

This is a specific form of end-state imagery where you visualize normalcy in your digestive system. White is a color of purity and health. You can elaborate on the imagery by visualizing symbolically the actual process of digestion, though it's not necessary. The mind will understand your intent either way.

Case illustration

The following case will illustrate how one patient used process imagery in his own weight loss program. It may help you construct similar imagery.

Mr. T, a middle-aged man weighing 235 pounds, was convinced that he was eating a "minimalist" diet, as he termed it, and yet could not lose weight. Thus, he had no motivation to decrease his food intake. Instead he decided to use process imagery to try to change the amount of food being digested and absorbed from his digestive system. Prior to starting his diet with me he had been on countless other diets where he would go through extreme periods of food curtailment including partial fasting for weeks at a time. His ability to lose weight slowly diminished, primarily I believe, from the slowdown of his basal metabolic rate. He came to understand the principle behind this potential change in his BMR as possibly causing some of his problems, but he was equally convinced that he had a genetic predisposition to periodic weight fluctuations beginning in childhood. He stated that he was never able to eat as much as other members of his family or other kids. By the time he was an adult he hardly ate and yet continued to gain weight unless he went on one of his periodic drastic diets.

At my suggestion he wrote in his journal everything he ate throughout the day. After two weeks it was certainly evident that his overall diet was consistent with his belief that he ate very little. Even taking into account some possible inaccuracy in his daily calorie count, he rarely ate more than 1,500 calories a day and many times it was as low as 1,200 calories. For his height of 5' 8", his weight, and his level of activity, which included mild exercise, he didn't have much leeway to reduce his diet further.

I believed that his limited diet might have come from his 20 or more diet attempts during the past two decades, many with extreme swings in weight. But I also agreed that his obesity during childhood suggested that he could indeed have an endocrine or other physiological condition that contributed to his weight problem. With this history, developing process imagery for his digestive system was warranted. It was added to other imagery he was using.

His objective was to cut down on what he assumed was an overactive digestive system that somehow over-digested the food he ate causing too much of it to be absorbed and converted into fat. Could such a thing happen? Possibly. If the amount of food he ate stayed longer in his stomach and small intestine than normal, one can conceive of a greater proportion of it being broken down and ultimately absorbed.

It's the opposite of what happens if someone has part of his stomach and small intestine surgically removed (gastric by-pass or gastric stapling) so that less food is eaten and spends less time in the small intestine being absorbed. Such persons tend to lose weight for the simple reason that they eat less and what they eat is not fully digested.

Mr. T created imagery to reduce food breakdown and absorption. He imagined all food that he put into his mouth as being very quickly transported down his esophagus and being pushed into his stomach by a piston apparatus. The food was not masticated nor changed when it settled in the stomach. Immediately small hollow steel balls, resistant to acid and digestive juices, gobbled the food up as fast as it appeared in the stomach. When all the food was trapped in the small globe-like traps, a derrick picked them up and placed them into a long cylinder powered like a rocket that shot through the small intestine in a matter of seconds, into the colon, and immediately ejected. During the process he had a sense of elation that he was defeating this part of his body that he believed was making him obese.

In addition he added imagery to boost his metabolic rate within his body by visualizing all muscles throughout his body becoming red hot and burning body fat. He imagined his body fat rapidly disappearing, literally consumed in front of his eyes. He felt no need to utilize imagery to prevent binge eating or excessive eating of any type since he truly ate very little for his body weight.

Finally, he added several kinds of end-state imagery. He imagined being normal weight and being admired by women. He saw himself becoming a great athlete even in his forties. He had always dreamed of engaging in various sports but felt his body size and difficulty in breathing would prevent it and also open him to ridicule. He choose tennis and golf as his sports, neither of which he played, but both of which would certainly be possible when he met his weight-loss goal.

He started a sustained exercise program at a gym. Because of his fear of over-exertion and possible heart problems he exercised under the guidance of a trainer. After three months I suggested he start on a twice-a-day exercise program to maintain the increased metabolic rate he was now achieving. He continued his expanded daily exercise for over eight months.

Six months after his diet had started, Mr. T, having gone through three diet months and three stabilization months, had lost 22 pounds, the highest amount he had been able to lose in the past six years. In earlier years he had gained and lost 30 to 50 pounds almost every year of his life, mainly through starvation diets.

He again wrote down every morsel of food he was eating during the day for a period of two weeks and discovered that his food intake was actually higher than indicated from his previous list. The reason for this became clear with a little investigation. Mr. T. had become quite knowledgeable about portion size and calorie content and was now more accurate in recording his daily food intake. Also there was a strong likelihood that he had managed to raise his normal metabolic rate somewhat due to his twice-a-day exercise program, as well as add some muscle bulk to his body.

He continued with his digestive system imagery which he felt had contributed to his successful dieting. He attributed his overcoming constipation and irregular bowel movements to the imagery. I believe that in addition to what the imagery offered, his increased use of high fiber foods and water was partially responsible for this change.

Imagery must fit your own concept of what will influence your eating habits. Use what you feel will work for you. Your belief in your imagery is crucial and your desire to change your behavior and physiological processes must remain strong and unrelenting. It's your belief that will change your thinking and behavior.

One of my patients asked how anyone could imagine a fire hose putting out the fire of a migraine headache. My response was that a patient who has felt an intense burning in the head from a migraine could easily imagine a hose spewing water on it. The same might be said for the woman who used a furnace to burn all the food in her stomach. She knew what "burning" in her stomach felt like, as do most of us. Relating that to a furnace is not difficult and can be believed. And if you can imagine food as poison or inedible, or disgusting, then vermin can become the symbol for those feelings.

PREMENSTRUAL SYNDROME (PMS)

Some of my diet patients who suffer from PMS elected to create imagery to fight the various symptoms related to their PMS. The complex nature of PMS requires a variety of imagery exercises directed to its symptoms. They rely on the belief that fluctuations in estrogen and progesterone just prior to the beginning of menstruation cause the symptoms. The imagery is strictly symbolic and assumes that bodily reactions can be modified. Since all my patients used the general imagery and other tools for dieting it is not clear how much of the improvement that occurred came from the PMS imagery. If you use these exercises I suggest you use them along with other imagery.

Many women have marked variations of their symptoms during the premenstrual period. The imagery should be practiced the entire month. Here are a few general ideas for developing imagery for PMS.

Imagine you are entering your PMS time period when you would normally anticipate suffering from a variety of symptoms. You can visualize each of your symptoms in symbolic form and immediately say you will no longer feel that symptom. For example, a headache could be visualized as a vise around your head or a hammer striking you repeatedly. You would visualize removing the vise or stopping the hammer and your pain immediately disappearing. You feel happy, calm, upbeat, in full control of your life and very positive. Believe that any symptoms you normally experience will not occur. Instead the opposite feelings would be felt.

Some of my patients use variations of the next two imagery exercises to attempt to control their PMS symptoms.

- Visualize yourself becoming agitated, depressed, emotionally unstable, or having whatever actual symptoms you have during your PMS period. Imagine a large X erasing the suffering you and being replaced by a calm person, totally free of your usual symptoms.
- Tie the decrease in your PMS symptoms to your loss of weight. See yourself becoming

thinner and thinner and your PMS symptoms disappearing with the fat that's also disappearing from your body.

OVERCOMING AN UNREALISTIC BODY IMAGE

Some people starting a diet have difficulty in establishing a reasonable body image as a goal for their diet. It's important that you overcome this idealization of your desired self since no diet will provide it. A few factors contributing to this idealization can be eliminated if recognized.

First is the need to admit any feeling of inferiority that is hidden behind the unrealistic picture of yourself when you have reached your desired weight. Most dieters in other programs rarely get to their desired weight before starting to regain weight. As they lose weight the obvious discrepancy of the real and idealized self sets up an impossible barrier. Out of frustration they begin to overeat again.

Second, you need to look at how you're influenced by models, advertisements, movies, etc. and repeatedly tell yourself that the influences are false and that you are beautiful yourself. The following imagery exercise is frequently helpful.

- Visualize yourself in the idealized body you desire and then slowly imagine it changing into a realistic and attractive body at the desired weight. Repeat that you love who you are, how you look, and that your real self is beautiful.

BINGE EATING DISORDER

Many overweight and obese people who compulsively

and rapidly eat large quantities of food two or more times a week are considered to be suffering from binge eating disorder. Binge eating has only recently been recognized as a form of compulsive overeating and is believed to be the most common form of eating problem. It occurs almost equally in women and men. The condition differs from bulimia nervosa, also characterized by recurrent episodes of binging, but which is accompanied by self-induced vomiting, purging with laxatives, and the use of diuretics. People with bulimia nervosa, which occurs primarily in young women, do not tend to gain weight.

Binge eating is characterized by a lack of eating control. Its symptoms include eating fast, eating until uncomfortably full, and hoarding. Binge eaters often eat alone and late at night due to embarrassment over the inability to stop eating, Feelings of guilt, disgust, and shame generally accompany it. Depression is a common finding in nearly half of binge eaters. Binge eating may go on for months or years. Excessive and often rapid weight gain and obesity are common but not always present.

Some binge eaters undertake brief, often desperate, periods of diet and exercise to gain temporary control over their weight. Such attempts cause rapid weight fluctuations. They do not use purge methods to control weight. Binge eaters often eat without feeling hungry.

It is estimated that over four million Americans have binge eating disorder. It is most common in the severely obese. However, all of them, including those who are simply overweight or even of normal weight can profit from the use of imagery and behavior techniques to control their eating.

Binge eating can lead to health complications that include heart disease, diabetes, high blood pressure, stroke, and some types of cancer.

Although no clear-cut physical or genetic cause has been discovered it has been noted that binge eaters tend to be sad and bored with their lives, worried about events and situations, and angry at their inability to control their eating. At times the use of cognitive-behavioral therapy or interpersonal psychotherapy brings some relief.

CONTROLLING BINGE EATING

Mental imagery exercises that focus on many of these underlying causes can help binge eaters overcome their need to do so. This special imagery doesn't take the place of imagery that is used for weight control. Gaining weight is more than just binge eating.

In each of the following exercises begin by visualizing yourself gorging on an enormous quantitiy of food.

- As rapidly as possible shovel food into your mouth. It can include all your favorites and literally anything you can get your hands on. At the moment of satiation, just as a big grin appears on your face, imagine yourself exploding. You scream in horror as you watch your body fly into millions of parts and all the food is scattered to the winds.
- As fast as possible your hands stuff food into your open and insatiable mouth. You have lost

> control of your eating. You can feel the food traveling through your intestines, into your colon, and in continuing explosive movements the food is shot out of your body. You are disgusted at your lack of control in both eating and defecating. You repeat to yourself over and over, *I want to stop binging!* Finally, you know that your mind is controlling your behavior and that you will no longer binge. You have gained control over your compulsion. The eating and defecation stop.

The nature of this imagery is not pleasant. But you need powerful imagery to help break this compulsion. Don't hesitate to make the imagery even more grotesque. Pour your feelings into the overeating and the catastrophic results. At the end of the imagery exercise repeat that your mind is growing more and more powerful and you are now in control of your overeating.

SIGNALING THE BRAIN TO STOP EATING

Although most of us have adequate supplies of leptin which signals the brain when sufficient food has been eaten, this imagery is to enhance that signal or provide a new signal. In addition to the stretch sensors in the stomach that signal the brain when it is filled, the level of blood glucose, and the presence of leptin in the fatty tissue, there are probably other signals. In overweight people these signals are not operating efficiently.

The following imagery should be added to your various physiological signals. This is a symbolic signal device. The body is fully aware of your intent and the feeling of fullness is activated psychologically.

- Imagine tiny sensory receivers and transmitters throughout the body that detect every molecule of fat and lipids, glucose, amino acids, and any other food ingredients that enter your body. Each time you eat, these receivers know exactly how much is appropriate for that meal or snack and sends an unequivocal message to the brain that you have eaten enough and it is time to stop. Tune into these messages during the imagery, listening as intently as possible. Play-act your ability to hear your body speak to you. Become aware that you can perceive the subtlest change within your body and know that you have developed another way of controlling your overeating. Tell yourself that the power of your mind is unlimited and is the source of the control over your eating.

RAISING YOUR BASAL METABOLIC RATE (BMR)

A patient who was eating very little food when she started her diet devoted her energy to raising her BMR. In addition to the twice a day exercise program that she began, she tried a number of imagery exercises to burn more calories.

When she had reached her desired weight a year and a half later, she had almost doubled the quantity of food she could eat without gaining weight. She had exercised a minimum of two hours a day, six days a week, during the entire period of her dieting and stabilization. The following is the imagery she selected from those she had created. Half of her total imagery time involved this one. She averaged, according to her journal entries, about 12 imagery sessions a day, each one being about two to three minutes long. She believed they contributed to her rather astounding results. I have used variations of this particular imagery with other patients.

- Visualize that all your fat stores have been ignited and are burning brightly. All floating molecules of fat and glucose are drawn to the fire and pour into the flaming fatty deposits. The fire immediately consumes them. You feel intense heat, similar to the elevated body heat you have felt during periods of intense exercise. You know with total conviction that your body is burning more calories every minute that your body is heated. You know that you are raising your basal metabolic rate. You tell yourself that your metabolic rate will remain higher for life.

OVERCOMING HUNGER

Can you stop the feeling of hunger? The answer is yes. There are a number of physiological sensors that warn a person when it's time to eat and when they've eaten enough. However, most overeaters ignore the signal that they are full.

Will stopping all feelings of hunger interfere with a proper diet and the enjoyment of food? Absolutely not. People who eat for pleasure are frequently not controlled by hunger. Their eating schedule is based on personal time schedules and the social interactions that accompany dining. Thus people might eat only once or as much as six times a day.

How then does one overcome hunger? We know that the genetic aspect of hunger involves the need to survive. Infants need to feel hunger pangs and act on them by crying. But as adults the survival component has essentially disappeared. We are left with strong psychological needs and social pressures. We all know that we need to eat to live. Hunger does not need to be felt to make us eat.

People who go on fasts tell us that once they've gone past the first few times that they normally eat they are rarely hungry again. If you want to overcome hunger the following imagery can help. The imagery is not done when you actually feel hungry but at other times during the day.

- Imagine that you feel very hungry. Exaggerate the hunger. Think of what you feel when hungry. Does your stomach growl? Do you salivate at the thought of food? Do you imagine sitting down at a table and indulging in your favorite foods? Do you feel real abdominal pain? Do you breathe heavier, perspire, or get anxious? Incorporate everything that means you are hungry into your imagery. Then exaggerate it wildly and emotionally. Feel extreme hunger. Play-act, if necessary. At the moment of the most intense hunger pangs say to yourself, "My mind is more powerful than even hunger and the pangs will now totally disappear." Immediately imagine that your hunger has gone. Exult, saying that your mind can do anything and you no longer will feel hunger.

Many of my patients successfully overcome or markedly lessen their feelings of hunger. Their enjoyment of eating is usually enhanced, but certainly never diminished. And it is not particularly difficult to achieve. As with all imagery it does take repetition and consistency.

Most people who overcome the feelings of hunger do not eliminate it completely. So when they go to a restaurant or dinner party they feel the desire to eat and look forward to the experience. This is quite different from being dominated by hunger and the compulsion to eat.

Overeating and the Need for Love

A frequent psychological problem faced by overeaters is their use of food to try to replace their need for love. If the compulsion to eat based on this love-food connection is very strong, psychotherapy may be necessary to help break the linkage. When the linkage is relatively weak it may be broken through the use of imagery.

Due to the nature of emotional conflicts and our ego defenses, imagery must be created with as much emotional intensity as possible. In the imagery exercises you should feel without any doubt that food is your substitute for love. When you see the food you feel the love. Then with even greater power you will break the linkage of this love-food connection. You know that food is not real love. Food makes you gain weight. You are going to stop using food for love. At times difficulties arise in creating imagery for psychological conflicts. You may not feel that you can make a believable connection between food and love. Don't be discouraged. By practicing these techniques you will eventually be able to make those connections with relative ease.

You may not feel worthy of being loved by yourself or by anyone and think you are constructing imagery that is false. You must keep in mind that the imagery is a force to combat the negative feelings in you. You create the imagery to overcome your negativity, much like the end-state imagery where you see yourself at your desired weight and feel empowered with a new sense of self.

If necessary, pretend you're an actor and can create any emotional state you desire. Don't feel that this kind of imagery is impossible to do. Reconditioning one's mind to new thoughts is part of self-growth. If imagery is new to you then you need time to understand its power and effect on your state of mind.

In the following imagery exercise you will discover that ultimately it is not food that gives you love. You give yourself love.

Loving yourself

- Visualize a large quantity of your favorite foods placed before you and imagine the gratification you will get by eating it. You are ravenously hungry. With fervor and exaggeration imagine a specific connection between the food and being loved. Imagine the food caressing or kissing you and trying to fill you with love. Then scream at the food. Tell it that it is false love. It makes you fat and unhealthy. Brush the food away with a flourish of your hand. Then put a large X across the food and turn your back on it. Hug yourself and feel that you are filling yourself with love. At the same time imagine that your hunger is diminishing.

Many of the overeaters who have this emotional linkage also have low self-esteem. Their self-confidence rises as they develop more self-love. Some of my patients actually hug themselves physically during the visualization.

Being loved by another person

At times it is beneficial to feel the love coming from someone other than yourself. For example, if it is clear that the lack of love stems from rejection by your mother or father or lover, the imagery can be used to imagine reconciliation taking place and being loved by that person. Use the same imagery as above and then choose the person who is to provide you with love.

You may want to visualize yourself as a child being hugged and kissed by the rejecting parent. If your overeating began with the rejection by a lover you can imagine being loved by another lover or even the same lover if the relationship is a continuing one.

One patient visualized being loved by God. Another patient used a favorite movie star. A number of my patients used a variety of alternating lovers. As you develop this type of imagery always remember that you are trying to reduce the connection between love and food. As you feel more loved, the use of food in place of love should diminish. As this happens you will be on your way to eliminating this particular stimulus for your compulsive eating. Diminishing or overcoming any psychological conflicts related to eating will improve your ability to control your weight.

DEPRESSION, ANXIETY, AND GUILT

Other negative feelings that relate to overeating can likewise be reduced. A good imagery technique for most emotional states is to first see yourself in that state of mind. Create an intense and highly exaggerated negative feeling. Then put a huge X across the negative you and replace it with a positive, happy, relaxed, and guilt-free you. Or make your negative self disappear in a cloud of smoke. Or imagine a great bird swooping down and carting your negative self off into the unknown. Whatever way you get rid of your negative self, do it with gusto and conviction.

The following example shows the use of imagery if you get depressed because you are overweight.

- Visualize yourself as the most depressed person in the world. Then plaster an enormous X across your depressed self. Visualize the X and your depressed self disappearing, followed immediately by a smiling, happy you. Visualize giving yourself a hug and saying how wonderful a person you are. At the same time reiterate that you are losing weight and gaining control over your excessive eating.

Use your imagination to construct imagery to help you reduce other psychological conflicts related to overeating. If you are beset with inferiority feelings, a sense of worthlessness, or feelings of ugliness, create imagery that will fight these negative attitudes.

Make yourself ugly beyond compare. Make yourself so ugly that your desire to eradicate that part of yourself will be overwhelming. Then use the same X to eradicate the ugly you. In its place create the most beautiful you that can be imagined. The more beautiful the better. Your beauty is internal and external. Real beauty is not in the shape of your nose or body, it is in the shape of your thoughts about yourself.

In your imagery you can become superman or superwoman, super attractive or super rich. You can have the power to move mountains. You no longer have to suffer from guilt or anxiety or any other negative feeling. Each time you do the exercises, create imagery that completely overcomes the negative feelings you have that are associated with overeating. Gradually, much as the basketball player slowly improves his shooting skills, your negative feelings should diminish and your self-esteem should rise.

Imagery works slowly and it is important that you don't expect to overcome all your negative attitudes after a few attempts at doing the exercises. Continuing motivation and persistence are necessary to change the deeply ingrained belief systems you currently have.

End-State Imagery

At the conclusion of your imagery exercises you should always use a variation of the following end-state imagery.

- Imagine yourself having the exact body size and weight that you desire. Be realistic. Look closely at your frame size and your muscle and fat distribution. Don't exaggerate the change you anticipate from your continuing exercise program. If your exercise consists primarily of walking, jogging, or cycling rather than bodybuilding with weights you should see your body as trim but without additional muscle development.

- Imagine yourself at your appropriate weight for your size and body type. See yourself looking and feeling attractive, alive, vital, and exuberant, sensing the joy in your body and in yourself.
- See yourself walking down the street or on the beach in a swimsuit attracting admiring glances. Walk swiftly with newfound energy.
- See yourself in athletic activities, more energetic and cheerful than before. Exult in the body that will someday be you.

Some of my patients only use end-state imagery to achieve permanent weight control.

CHOICE OF IMAGERY

What governs the choices of imagery each dieter makes? There is no easy answer. Some will find that the imagery described in this book satisfies their needs. Others will need to create totally original imagery. Others mix and frequently change their imagery. Some use only negative imagery; some only positive. It makes no difference what imagery you select if you believe it fits your particular problem. Whether you use literal, symbolic, process, or end-state imagery also makes no difference.

Above all, don't let personal feelings about the negative imagery turn you off from using any imagery. A number of my patients found negative imagery unacceptable and chose not to include them. This did not interfere with their gaining permanent weight control. The ability to overcome negative belief systems is the key to weight control. The case histories will show more clearly how negative imagery can be incorporated into diet programs.

Hypnotists will tell you that when they use imagery for healing it matters little what symbols they use. The person being hypnotized believes in the power of the hypnotist to influence his beliefs provided it doesn't interfere with his moral or ethical values.

Likewise, if you believe in your selection of imagery, it will work for you. You will probably recognize an intuitive element at work in your selection. The imagery may appear spontaneously and feel absolutely right. Or a number of visualizations may appear and you select one by eliminating all the others that do not seem right. This process may include both intuition and the use of logical and rational thinking. Learn to trust both of these faculties of your mind. Your desire to overcome your weight problem and the belief in the power of your mind to change your thinking will ultimately bring you success.

CHAPTER FIFTEEN

Relapse

Few compulsive eaters are able to undergo a diet program and continue it without periods of relapse. Relapse can last for one day or several months. It may occur without any apparent cause. A dieter suddenly gets the impulse to binge or overeat for a period of time. Sometimes the relapse is triggered by emotional stress. Usually the stress develops from certain psychological stimuli related to their emotional conflicts.

It makes no difference what causes the relapse. It should be considered a signal that you need to reestablish contact with your inner self and try to determine the cause. The journal will facilitate this process. Reexamine your imagery and change or modify those that no longer appear to be helping. Resume your diet program if the relapse occurred during a diet month. If it occurs in a stabilization month strive to reduce your food intake and return to the same weight you had established at the beginning of the month.

Some overweight persons start their diet without using the imagery. However, if you find that there is a tendency to relapse frequently, especially for long periods of time, then you need to consider using imagery exercises as part of your diet program. If the relapse was for only one meal, rely on drinking extra water to get rid of the extra pounds.

Relapse is never to be taken as the end of your dieting. It should always be considered a prelude to resuming the program—never to stopping it. This diet and weight control program has worked for many people and can work for you. Do everything possible to overcome any negative beliefs that stand in the way of accomplishing your goal.

Developing new belief systems takes time. Put yourself on a reasonable time schedule. Do not hesitate to modify your monthly goals. Make your weight loss routine easy, even pleasant. There is no need to starve yourself or develop guilt over temporary relapses. You can even have fun creating the imagery.

Remember that achieving weight control leads to other benefits in addition to the improvement in your general health. Your self-esteem, your sense of youthfulness, and your joy at being alive will be enhanced.

Many people who diet believe that they can never again eat normally, that they will never fully enjoy the uninhibited pleasures of dining without the fear of losing control and gaining weight. Such negative thoughts frequently undermine any weight control method. However, by following the concepts introduced in this book you should ultimately be able to eat anything you want in normal amounts without regaining the lost weight.

The primary objective of this program is to help you gain permanent control over your eating habits so that you never again have to go on a strict diet.

As we proceed you will discover the ways to enjoy

all foods, indulge yourself when the desire calls, and never gain weight. This control is accomplished by the continuing use of water, the scale, exercise, and mental imagery exercises.

When you finally reach your goal of permanent weight control your dieting will have ended and it will be the beginning of a new way of life. Maintain the five primary components of your diet program indefinitely for they will have become part of how you live. The stabilization period will have reached permanent status.

The imagery can be done a few minutes a day as a reminder and motivating force of your continuing self-control. By maintaining a healthy diet and continuing to exercise you will have incorporated into your life two essential elements for enduring vitality and aliveness. You will be at the beginning of a richer, more vital, and happier existence.

CHAPTER SIXTEEN

The Journal

Why keep a journal? Because it will enhance your ability to lose weight and, more important, to keep it off forever. My patients who had experienced many years of yo-yo dieting benefited greatly from the use of a journal.

You may have been looking for a solution to your weight problem for a long time. Now is the time to commit yourself as fully as possible to using the techniques of the *Five Keys* program. These techniques work, but they're not automatic. They require effort, time, and continuing motivation.

Think how often you may procrastinate in doing something you are ambivalent about. Whether you decide to become a long-distance runner, or improve your skills in tennis or golf, or learn to play the piano, or clean out the garage, or undergo another diet, it is easy to postpone doing it. It is equally easy to start the project and not continue, finding one excuse after another not to resume. It is not easy to overcome this tendency that we all have, but I want to help you face this issue now. You want to diet and feel healthy, to live well and enjoy life more fully. That should be your rallying cry as you probe into any resistance that comes up.

The journal serves a very valuable purpose. It will help you focus on the kinds of things that you will face during your dietary period. A journal, like a diary, is a work in progress. You can record your deepest fears, frustrations, and any doubts about the program or your ability to maintain your motivation. You can keep tabs on what you eat and what causes relapses. You can unburden yourself of your experiences that cause suffering. And you can also tell about your dreams and hopes. The journal provides a way of looking into your inner world and offers you a glimpse of parts of you that you may not have known.

Your journal can be your confidant. You can pour your deepest feelings into it. It is only for your eyes and thus there is no need to hide anything from it. In a way a journal can become like an intimate companion.

It would be the rare person who sails through this program without periods of doubt or relapsing or boredom or a belief that it's a waste of time. These are the kinds of feelings you need to face and overcome. This program is based on established principles, both physiological and psychological, and will work for you. But it must be pursued and used as indicated. Questions, doubts, and successes, too, find expression in the journal.

One of the areas that I'm almost always questioned about is the stabilization period. When you have just lost six or more pounds in a month and are feeling excited by the prospect of continuing to lose weight, your motivation tends to be high. You're on a fast track toward reaching your goal and it may be hard to stop in midstream and stabilize your weight for an entire month. But the stabilization period offers more than just preventing your BMR from decreasing and giving you periods to adjust to your reduced weight. It's also a time for reflection and the journal is your helper.

The journal can be an instrument to improve your use of the program. It will help you examine your eating habits, stress factors, and any psychological elements that may contribute to your overeating. It is helpful to ask yourself why you believe you are overweight. What types of stress stimulate you to eat? Why can't you, a disciplined person, apply that discipline to your eating?

The journal also provides a creative outlet for new ways of using imagery that go beyond dieting. It offers you a way of keeping track of your imagery selections and when and why you change them. As you go through different phases of your dieting, your selection of imagery will most likely change, sometimes markedly. By examining your thinking behind these changes you will discover new aspects of your eating habit. Such insight will improve your weight control techniques.

If you relapse, your journal allows you to go back and trace patterns to see where the triggers for relapse may have occurred. You can use it weekly, daily, or several times a day. You can make it into whatever you want.

The journal will become a vehicle to foster personal growth. The following questions will help you focus on different aspects of your struggle to lose weight and develop weight control.

GENERAL QUESTIONS FOR SELF-AWARENESS

- Why are you overweight?
- What specific stress factors contribute to your overeating? Do they involve people, work, boredom, loneliness, or other concerns? Can you reduce this stress?
- Does being overweight serve some hidden purpose, like avoiding meeting people, not wanting to exercise, or supporting feelings of inferiority? If so, describe this hidden agenda.
- If you have had periods of normal weight alternating with being overweight, list the reasons for these fluctuations.
- To the best of your ability list the approximate number of calories you normally eat and what proportion of fat, carbohydrates, and protein you consume.
- Do you need only to reduce the amount of normal food you eat or do you primarily need to reduce the amount of fat or sugar you consume?
- Do you require others to prepare the food you expect to use on your diet? If so, list the reasons you are dependent on someone else having a controlling influence in your diet.
- What genetic or medical factors, if any, may be contributing to your overeating? Do you believe they set a limit to your weight loss or increase your difficulty in establishing and maintaining

a reasonable diet? If so, what mental changes do you have to make to ensure your continuing motivation in developing weight control?

- What are the attitudes and feelings of family members and friends toward your weight control attempts? Do they support your efforts? Are there ways to improve their support, if needed?
- Are you self-motivated? Are you more effective when working in groups or with other forms of external support? What can you do to improve your belief in your individual power to develop weight control?
- Is your overeating influenced by others? If so, how can you gradually diminish this influence so that you become fully responsible for your food intake?

IMAGERY

Like dreams, it is sometimes hard to remember imagery settings and exercises. The journal helps you keep track of them as well as how and why you change them. It often helps to reflect on why you choose your particular imagery. The insight gained by this introspection offers added understanding of your eating compulsion, which in turn, increases your motivation to reach your goal of complete weight control.

Imagery can arouse much emotion and frequently taps into conscious and subconscious conflicts that are difficult to face. Any evidence that you are avoiding the use of imagery should be quickly examined and noted in your journal. Try and evaluate what negative beliefs are interfering with your use of the imagery. Once you write it down you have already taken a major step to overcoming it. Each day continue to use the journal to note your progress in fighting this resistance.

At times the resistance is disguised by using various excuses and subterfuges. The following are some you should look out for.

- You think that you do not have enough time to practice the imagery.
- You don't believe your mind can change your behavior.
- You have inner doubts that you can develop the necessary self-control to change your behavior.
- You find it difficult to accept the concept of self-empowerment.
- You stop doing the imagery after a few weeks because it doesn't seem to be working.
- You have difficulty in putting much enthusiasm into creating your imagery and begin to find it boring.
- You have ambivalence toward dieting. You have a conflict in giving up the amount of eating you engage in.

The journal acts like a diary to record your reflections about yourself and your life. In this case the focus is on your diet. As you develop imagery to combat your eating compulsion, your self-awareness tends to increase. Be alert to any negative elements that you perceive in yourself that in any way contributes to your overeating. Be especially sensitive to any connection between overeating and feeling unloved and to feelings of rejection, loneliness, inferiority, self-condemnation, depression, and anxiety.

It is not easy to face negative feelings in ourselves but our efforts will be well rewarded. As you begin to understand your diet-related imagery you will learn more about your feelings and behavior in other areas as well. Your self-esteem and self-awareness will be enhanced. A general feeling of well-being and increased self-respect will improve all aspects of your life.

If you need to change any of your imagery, examine why. What did you learn about your eating compulsion and your inner self based on the change of imagery?

WATER

It sometimes helps to construct a simple chart of water usage, at least in the early phase of your dieting. The amount of water you think you're drinking may be much less than it should be. Charting it will help you see whether you are drinking an adequate amount of water on a daily basis.

The dietary use of water is a life-long technique that becomes a permanent part of your continuing weight control. During the initial period when you are adapting water to your diet there may be marked fluctuations in your water use without your conscious awareness. By using a simple chart you can develop added discipline to your diet program.

If you are resistant to using water for weight control, note the reasons in your journal. Write down how you can overcome this resistance. Never accept resistance as a reason to not use a component of your diet or to stop the program. By working to overcome the resistance you are establishing important links to your self-empowerment and control over your behavior.

It's also useful to keep track of your use of the special extra water diet when you have gained any weight. How many glasses of water were necessary to lose specific amounts of weight? How effective was the special diet in reducing your weight to the weight level of the previous day? You will be able to detect variations in the timing and frequency of the water diuresis. In general, it happens in one day, but occasionally it takes two days for the extra water to be excreted with its salt content. The effectiveness of the extra water is sometimes delayed during the diet month due to the homeostatic mechanisms, but you will lose the weight. Your body physiology is on your side. Its effectiveness during the stabilization period is more precise.

THE SCALE

Record in your journal your daily weight during the first month of your diet, using the scale as your psychological assistant. Note reactions to weight increases if they occur. Do you react to increases of weight with enthusiasm instead of anger or self-condemnation? It is essential that you overcome any negative reactions to weight gain. This assures that you will develop the discipline to weigh yourself daily and benefit from the special extra water diet if needed. People who fear gaining weight tend to avoid the scale.

Another benefit comes from keeping track of the

time when weight is decreasing versus those inevitable periods of homeostasis when the body tries to retain water to maintain body weight. Having the weight recorded allows you to see patterns in your weight loss. At times a dieter will lose a few pounds and then without going off his diet regain it. This happens due to the homeostatic mechanism that influences body weight.

Homeostasis, the mechanism of equilibrium and stability, is a normal function of our bodies. Our bodies attempt to prevent weight change even though we have dropped calories and lost fat pounds. It does so by temporarily decreasing urine output and retaining fluid. But eventually all excess water is eliminated through a temporary increase in urine output. You may suddenly see a drop of several pounds. If the homeostatic control center hasn't fully adapted to your new weight you may quickly regain that lost weight. Don't despair. Ultimately the body mechanisms catch up with your actual weight loss.

THE STABILIZATION PERIOD

It is important that you maintain the weight you achieve at the end of each month of dieting during each subsequent month of stabilization. By recording the increasing number of calories you eat each day during the stabilization period you will come to appreciate your growing control over your food intake. Many people on diets who have reached their desired weight are afraid to consciously eat more than they did when dieting. Their fear of regaining weight is a major deterrent. You, on the other hand, are doing this deliberately and thereby gaining increased confidence in your ability to control your weight.

In your journal, list your weight at the end of the month's dieting and note the average number of calories you ate each day of your diet. Then at the end of your stabilization month note the number of calories or the quantity of food you are eating that is above the calorie count at the end of your diet month. You will learn how much added food you need to maintain your new monthly weight and therefore how much food you can tolerate without regaining weight.

For example, let's say you calculate that you were on a 1,200-calorie diet during the month of dieting. At the end of the month of stabilization you calculate you were eating 1,700 calories. You would register the 500-calorie difference between the diet month and the end of the stabilization month. Most dieters need one or two weeks each stabilization period to determine how much food is required to maintain their new weight.

Your confidence in gaining mastery over your weight will grow enormously during the stabilization periods when you eat a relatively normal diet without gaining or losing weight. You will continue to use all the other parts of your diet program during the stabilization month and will keep track of any resistance to their use.

Do not become discouraged if at first you are unable to maintain your exact weight during the stabilization period. Just honestly analyze why you regained weight and apply your energy to continuing the program. There is no reason to feel guilty or inadequate due to occasional lapses in control. The control you are seeking does not come overnight. But by sticking to this program you will achieve permanent weight control. Be patient and believe in yourself.

Expect some minor weight fluctuation during stabilization as the body adjusts to your new weight, but always strive to return to the precise weight you had attained at the beginning of the month. When you have reached your desired weight any upward change is to be viewed as water retention (assuming there was no massive binging) and can be handled by the extra water diet. For example, if your desired weight is 130 pounds and on one day you gained three pounds you would initiate the special water diet and drink an extra 4½ glasses of water that day (three glasses per two pounds) to return to 130 pounds the following day.

If one day you awakened and your weight was 127 pounds you would assume you had lost more water than normal (heat loss, exercise loss, sweating under any circumstance). On this one day you would eat an additional 600 calories or sprinkle some additional salt on your food and drink 4½ glasses of extra water to regain the lost three pounds.

EXERCISE

Exercise helps you lose weight by burning more calories during and after each exercise period. In addition, it serves a greater purpose. Exercise helps create a healthier body, a new sense of youthfulness, and feelings of vitality. Exercise increases stamina, alertness, and one's ability to relax.

If you are just beginning to add exercise to your program it is helpful to record the time, the kind, and the amount of exercise you undergo during each week. If you are already on a regular exercise program you may not need to keep a record of it.

Exercise should be fun. Negative feelings toward exercise require careful evaluation in order to overcome any tendency to stop this part of your program. Don't let the fact that the diet works whether or not you exercise keep you from doing it. The health benefits are many and go far beyond helping you diet and maintain your weight.

Some people like to write down their reactions to various types of exercise. It becomes a place to record their feelings about training for a marathon, or riding their bike into a new and beautiful area, or reaching a feeling of tranquility or excitement.

Some dieters prefer to continue recording weight changes throughout their entire diet as part of their discipline and motivation. Experiment. Above all this is a time to trust your judgment as you modify any aspects of your diet program. There is no actual time limit for you to reach your weight destination. You are setting up a life-long method of weight control that will finally remove the burden of yo-yo dieting from your life.

CHAPTER SEVENTEEN

Case Histories

To protect the identity and privacy of the patients whose case histories I've used, I have made changes in ages, situations, circumstances, and places, but the facts remain unaltered. I have also taken some liberties with dialogue to allow the patient to become more alive in my presentation.

These particular patients presented a variety of dietary problems that, while unique, are similar to those we all face. The imagery each patient developed shows the wide range of choices available to you.

Most of these patients were imaginative in their use of imagery and several had unusual cases that required exceptional creativity. But in no case was there anything unusual in how these patients used the diet program and the imagery.

All of these patients eventually used imagery for other needs and interests besides dieting. I always encourage this for it provides a new way of looking at life and at ourselves. It also provides ways of changing other kinds of behavior that ultimately improves weight control.

RACHEL: SAYING GOODBYE TO ERNIE

Rachel was everyone's mother. Her first visit was a family affair. Two pleasant-looking women accompanied Rachel into my office and introduced themselves as Marcia and Judith, her daughters. Rachel was very obese and was having some difficulty in walking. Her daughters, though not obese, were certainly considerably overweight. As soon as Rachel sat down, assisted by her daughters, she looked directly at me. A warm smile came to her face despite her labored breathing.

"Doctor, I hope you don't mind that my daughters came with me. I'm not breathing too well and they were afraid I might have trouble getting here."

Rachel spoke very slowly. Her words were expressed in short gasps of air as she told me her history. Rachel was 67 years old and had been overweight all her adult life. She currently weighed 210 pounds and at 5' 2" was close to double her optimal weight. She had attempted many diets over the years and fluctuated between 170 and 210 pounds. Her weight was now at its highest ever and slowly rising.

During the past year she had gained ten pounds and had developed a variety of medical problems that brought deep concern to her family. The list of symptoms was very familiar to me. They were present in many older overweight people. Shortness of breath, impending heart failure, hypertension, increasing osteoporosis, varicose veins, lethargy, elevated blood sugar, and the beginning of Type 2 diabetes, to name a few. Rachel appeared to be a walking medical text of symptomatology.

Her family doctor who knew of my work with obesity had called to indicate his concern about her heart and a recent abnormal EKG, as well as her developing diabetes. He felt she needed counseling to try to stop her current eating spree and continuing weight gain. She had stopped all exercise and had become housebound.

Rachel's husband, Ernie, had died of a heart attack a year earlier, which apparently was the stimulus for her recent weight gain. Rachel indirectly confirmed my observation as she talked about how difficult it had been to adjust to his sudden death. He was only 71 when he died.

On close questioning it appeared that Rachel and Ernie had a warm and loving relationship during their 43 years of marriage. She had never established a strong independent side, preferring to be guided by her husband's interests and needs.

Despite the attentiveness of her two daughters and the closeness to her four grandchildren she felt lonely and depressed. Finding it difficult to engage in social situations alone and too tired to maintain contact with her many friends, she began to use food to satisfy her feeling of emptiness. This is not an uncommon occurrence during the period of grieving for the loss of a loved one.

Rachel described her lifelong concern with obesity. "I've always been heavy. I enjoy food and love to cook for my family and, although I have tried a number of diets, I never thought being heavy was a real problem for me. My husband and my children loved me and my being heavy didn't seem to disturb anyone. But I'm now concerned about my medical problems."

Marcia interrupted, "We are, too. As you can tell, Mom has trouble breathing even when talking, but she wanted to tell you her story."

Rachel continued. "My children insisted that I come here today and go on another diet. My doctor says that unless I lose weight he has no choice but to start me on insulin."

On questioning I found little relevant information about her essentially middle-class social and family life. I had little doubt that her family life before the death of her husband was nurturing and satisfying. "I loved my husband very much," she had told me. "Our relationship was very close."

When I asked whether the death of her husband contributed to her having gained the last ten pounds, she immediately answered in the affirmative. "I was very unhappy when Ernie died and I imagine that eating more food was a way of bearing my grief."

With Rachel's need to rapidly lose weight I decided that she would start her diet without the use of mental imagery. She seemed highly motivated and her daughters would be very supportive of the program. I would determine the need for imagery at a later time.

Marcia took notes as I described the program. She indicated that she would also follow it. Judith smilingly said, "I will, too. We'll make it a family affair."

"Very often having the entire family start the diet together helps everyone to maintain it," I said.

We agreed to meet again in three weeks. They were to start the diet at the beginning of the following month which was six days away. They would keep journals and record their daily weight, the amount of water they drank, and the amount of time and effort expended in their exercise programs. Rachel would discuss with her medical doctor what level of exercise was possible at this time and follow his advice. We also reviewed the ingredients of a balanced diet and the importance of eating foods containing less fat and refined sugars.

Three weeks later Rachel and her two daughters came to their scheduled appointment. All three had started their diets and only Rachel had not lost weight. Her family doctor, concerned with her impending heart failure, did not wish her to exercise until she began to lose weight.

Rachel apologized for her inability to stay on the diet. She said, "Whenever I think of Ernie I just want to eat. I can't help it. I go to the cupboard and find some nuts or bread or anything." She struggled to hold back her tears. Wheezing from her chest was audible. Her heart medication was only partly effective. She needs to lose weight soon, I thought.

I introduced Rachel and her daughters to mental imagery. Rachel's eyes lit up as I explained the power of imagery and how it enables the mind to overcome negative beliefs. I emphasized how imagery can give a person a new sense of freedom and increased self-control. Rachel appeared ready to start. For the first time during this visit she smiled and her blue eyes seemed to sparkle. She had grasped the essential value of visualization and immediately believed that she would learn how to control her mind.

During her first imagery session we created the following three exercises.

- She visualized nailing the cupboard doors shut and placing a large placard on the door that simply said, *Stay out! You are not to open this door for food.* The letters were large, bold, and in red. Rachel was to repeat the words, "Opening that door is strictly forbidden!"

- Whenever she felt lonely and reached for food, it would suddenly vanish. Simultaneously a large piece of adhesive tape would cover her mouth. A voice would shout at her, "You are not to eat any extra food again." When she agreed to that prohibition the tape would come off her mouth.
- In an imagery exercise that involved her dependency she would visualize dressing up in pretty clothes and venturing forth to a social event to meet friends. She would see herself as warm, smiling, and energetic. People would gather around her.

She immediately adapted to the rag doll relaxation technique and promised to do each of the three imagery exercises a minimum of 12 times a day. She would also continue her diet until the end of the month. The stabilization month would follow no matter how much weight she lost, even if it were zero. Her daughters were to generate their own imagery exercises at home.

Rachel arrived with both daughters again. She was beaming as she told me she had lost four pounds in two weeks. Then she grew quiet and finally said in a soft sad voice, "I think I need to free myself from Ernie. He would want me to. One night, about a week after we last saw you, I dreamed that Ernie was waving at me from a train that was leaving the station. I don't know much about dreams, but I knew as soon as I awakened that Ernie was saying good-bye to me. I knew then that I must finally say good-bye to him. Only then will I know that he rests in peace."

Although Rachel again became quiet, I waited. Tears appeared in her eyes as she spoke. "For several days I cried while thinking of saying goodbye to Ernie but I knew I had to do it. I made up a new imagery by myself. I knew he had to leave."

The imagery, so simple, but so meaningful, told the story. "Ernie and I walk together to the train station. He gets on the train alone. As the train pulls out of the station I see him waving from a window. I start to cry and then I wipe my tears and I also wave good-bye and tell him I'll always love him no matter where he is. I know that he's gone from my life, but not from my heart."

Rachel paused, then again spoke, her voice broken by sobs. "I start all my imagery sessions with saying good-bye to Ernie. Every day I do it over and over. It's so hard but I know it's what Ernie wants me to do. I love him so much."

Rachel now openly cried and Marcia took her in her arms. My heart went out to her as she described the imagery. I knew that Rachel had taken her first real step toward independence.

During the next year I continued to see Rachel once a month. One or both daughters always accompanied her. She expanded her use of imagery in all areas of her life and did the sessions six to twelve times a day. Each session contained several exercises and incorporated a variety of themes.

One involved strengthening her heart, clearing her lungs of fluid, and overcoming her wheezing. She imagined becoming tiny enough to enter her own body, traveling into her lungs, and with a mechanical pump removing the fluid and all debris she found there. She knew her lungs were now well and she would soon breathe normally. She then entered her heart and by touch alone brought strength to it. I told her that these were wonderful visualizations since she was providing her own strength to restore her health.

Another visualization played out her tendency to overeat when at a friend's house. Her need to accept a friend's hospitality included eating too much. She learned through her imagery how to say, "No, thank you," without guilt or fear of offending anyone. In her imagery she first told her friends "No, thank you" in a warm and kind voice. But within a few weeks she laughingly told me she was imagining screaming at her friends for daring to offer her food and knocking the food out of their hands. Her imagery was becoming more emotional, exaggerated, and expressive.

Another visualization strengthened her resolve to exercise and go to a gym three times a week.

Adding an end-state image of how she would look when she finished her dieting was surprisingly more difficult. But it allowed me to understand an inner negative belief system that needed to be changed. She still had doubts that she could one day weigh 120 pounds, her realistic goal. I convinced her that with her newfound strength, staying with her diet, and finding new imagery exercises to maintain her motivation, she would eventually reach her goal. She finally began to imagine herself young looking, slender, and very attractive. She would pretend she was a teenager wiggling her hips and acting coquettish to men. The staid and sober Rachel was seeing herself as a flirt.

Rachel came to see me for three years. Her daughters rarely came during the last year but Rachel always told me of their progress. Both Marcia and Judith had reached their desired weight in the early part of the second year of their dieting and had established permanent weight control.

On her last visit Rachel informed me that she had run her second 10K marathon and was only one of four people in their 70s who accomplished it. She had reached 120 pounds and I truthfully told her she looked 20 years younger. Her reply was, "I may look 20 years younger, but I feel 50 years younger."

She promised to write me from time to time. And so she did for almost twelve years. When she died I felt I had lost a part of myself. But she had left me with the memory of her dazzling blue eyes, her warm and loving smile, and her heart that she shared so freely with the world.

GEORGE: LOVE, HATE, AND OBESITY

George was 36, tall, moderately obese, good-looking, and articulate. He sat facing me and immediately glued his eyes to mine. Within five minutes I began to feel uncomfortable by the intensity of his staring. Even when I deliberately looked away for a few moments his eyes never left the spot where he knew my eyes would return. George appeared compelled to make eye contact. I wondered how this was related to his coming to see me.

George had been a star athlete in high school and college. On graduation from college he appeared to be heading for a career in professional baseball. Shortly after he was picked by a team in the National League, George started to eat uncontrollably. He said it happened so suddenly that it took him by surprise. He had no idea why it occurred.

The source of his compulsion began to emerge as he told me his story. When George was six his parents got divorced. Initially he divided his time equally between his mother and father. As he grew older he spent more and more time with his father who began to groom him for a career in baseball. His father had become aware of George's great talent and potential future in professional sports.

An only child, George commanded his father's constant attention and enjoyed a close relationship with him. In high school George reached the status of a baseball deity. "I could do no wrong. Everyone wanted to be my friend. I could pitch or play outfield or first base. Anything they wanted I could do better than anyone else. I was called the next Mickey Mantle." By the time he finished college he was being sought by numerous professional ball clubs and ended up signing a lucrative contract.

"I never had any trouble with food or weight or anything like that," George assured me. "But I began to eat like crazy as soon as I was supposed to go to the minor league team. That was fourteen years ago." George now paused, though he still stared at me.

"What happened then?" I prompted him.

"My baseball career never started. I couldn't stop eating. The team had me see a psychologist and then a psychiatrist. Nothing helped. I took pills and got sick. I ballooned out to nearly 100 pounds over my normal weight. I never even suited up. Everyone thought something terrible had happened to me. They even thought I had a brain tumor. The day I was let go I went into hiding, and only then was I able to stop my crazy eating. But I continued to eat too much and was never able to lose all the weight I'd gained. Every couple of years I would again get this terrible urge to eat. I ate like a starving monkey. At one time I was almost 150 pounds overweight. Then I'd get control and lose weight. And it's been like that all these years. Right now I'm in my mid-range at about 275 pounds."

Acting on a hunch I looked down toward the floor and then back up. George's eyes were still there. "George, are you aware that you're staring at me?" I asked.

"No, am I staring at you?" George appeared flustered.

"Yes," I responded, "but I don't believe you've been aware of it. Has anyone ever mentioned something similar to you?"

"Why yes, many times, but I always thought they were kidding. Everyone knows I'm a straightforward guy who is totally trustworthy and people really like me. I always thought that looking someone in the eye was showing how direct I am."

"When did people first mention it to you?"

For the first time George looked away and thought a few moments before he spoke. "I think it was in high school. Girls used to say I was creepy the way I looked at them, even though they treated me like a hero. I took it as a joke."

"Was this true of all girls?"

George thought carefully before he answered. "No.

I think it mainly happened with girls I liked. Other girls never said anything. I shrugged it off. I could always find another girl if someone didn't like me."

By the time George entered high school his father had essentially taken over his life. He not only guided his athletic development, he scrutinized everything George did.

"My father was everywhere," George said. "I couldn't even go to the bathroom without his coming in to talk to me. I felt like I was never alone."

In college the head coach welcomed his father's willingness to assist with the coaching. And for four years his father continued to watch everything he did.

"He never took his eyes off me," George said. "My father gave up most of his friends. He never dated or saw women. I became all he needed. My life was not my own. But the worst thing that happened was my father's arranging to become a paid assistant for the minor league team. His reputation had grown and was tied to me. Everyone was aware that he was my primary coach and he would never hesitate to spout off about his knowledge of baseball. Even going to the National League would not free me from my father. I was desperate and even thought of leaving the country. I would have done anything to stop him from coming with me."

"Anything?" I asked.

"Yes, anything."

"Anything?" I said a second time.

And that was the moment that George began to understand the cause behind his compulsive eating. Over many years he harbored deep resentment toward his father for interfering with his independence. "My father was suffocating me," he said, angrily.

His unexpressed anger toward his father during his teens and early twenties was converted to defeating his father's efforts to make him a star. Becoming a non-athlete was his unwitting choice.

No athlete succeeds who is obese. George's over-eating served several purposes. It defeated his father. It also sabotaged his own wish to be a star. George felt extremely guilty about his unexpressed anger, and becoming obese served as his personal punishment.

George was now ready to begin his diet. He would start using all five components of the program. Despite his great athletic ability he had not exercised in years. He immediately began an exercise program. He understood the value of the scale and the specific way water was to be used. Initially, the imagery was to be directed at his general eating habits which, except for the periodic compulsive and explosive binge eating, involved overeating at meal times. He rarely ate between meals even when binging.

The imagery for his mealtime overeating involved visualizing himself knocking the food off the table with a single sweep of his arm. "What isn't in front of me I don't eat" was his rationale for this simple imagery. It sufficed.

He added end-state imagery of himself wearing a baseball uniform and at his prime weight before his first compulsive binging at the age of 22. He believed that he must accept himself that way despite his feelings toward his father. He later added playing various positions on a major league team and being lauded by fans. He was trying to undo the last fourteen years of self-hate and regret.

The imagery to overcome his binging and diminish the influence of his father on his weight problem was anything but simple. It took several months to develop an effective series of imagery exercises to begin to chip away at his eating compulsion. Together we searched for hidden feelings and meanings in his thinking and behavior. Entries in his journal, which he made daily, facilitated his understanding. Slowly he uncovered the specific conflicts that triggered his compulsive eating. They became the basis to both overcome his eating problem and his untenable relationship with his father.

By his third month of using the diet and imagery, George established a series of powerful visualizations that helped him control his eating compulsion. After a number of experimental imagery exercises George settled on the following ones.

- He visualized his father shaped like a snake leaping at him and taking large bites from his head and skull. His snake-father then forced himself into his brain and then slipped into his mind. George screamed and with great effort pulled his father from his head and smashed him to bits. He exulted, knowing he had removed his father from his mind.
- He was being shackled to his father by a long chain. His father pulled him at will wherever he wanted. George then picked up a large baseball bat and moved toward his father. His father picked up his own bat and they began a mighty struggle for supremacy. The two combatants moved back and forth over the entire earth as they fought to the death. Finally, George, in a

supreme effort and with a mighty blow, splintered his father's bat and proceeded to smash him into the ground. With one final blow he broke the chain that attached him to his father and knew that he was free at last.

- He was sitting down at a table of food with his father watching every bite. Every few moments his father would scream that he's eating too much. George calmly grabbed his father and taped his mouth tightly closed, telling him to keep his mouth shut. "I'll eat as much as I want. I know when to stop and I don't need you to tell me what and how much to eat."
- He was playing baseball in a major league game and making great plays, hitting home runs, and seeing his father in the stands waving and shouting his approval. For this imagery George was now able to accept his father's pleasure in his abilities without any sense of being controlled or feeling angry. He kept his father at a distance in the stands and forgave his attempts to control his life. He felt his guilt and hate for his father disappear until he was finally free of imprisonment by his father.

In these imagery exercises George attempted to change various mindsets that he carried much of his life. His belief that his father had usurped his independence underwent change. He used symbolic imagery to extricate his father from his inner thoughts. He was able to express his intense anger at his father and fear of his disapproval. His guilt and need for punishment as well as his struggle to separate from his father were directly confronted. The fears he carried with him from childhood were examined and slowly overcome through his repeated symbolic defeat of his father.

With the advent of this new freedom he was able to forgive his father and forgive himself for his anger at a father who he also loved. As he became his own person he no longer needed to maintain his compulsive eating and obesity.

The case study of George represents the way that mental imagery can be used to overcome or minimize deep-seated conflicts that influence obesity.

I saw George twelve times over a period of six months during which time he lost 17 pounds. He kept in contact with me for over two more years as he slowly lost weight, averaging five or six pounds each diet month. His goal was reached 2½ years from the date he began his diet program.

This case also illustrates how motivation to change behavior has many vicissitudes and can't be measured only in weight loss or time required. When George wrote me the last time, he said, "I need to express my deep appreciation for helping me change myself and overcome not just a weight problem but a problem in my soul. I had lived impoverished and unfulfilled. I saw myself as a failure and unable to find a way out.

"The imagery went beyond just a series of pictures in my mind. Those pictures taught me new ways to think and to live. Each pound of weight that I lost also represented the lifting of a pound of mental suffering. Each time I created another imagery exercise I also discovered a lost part of myself.

"The last year has been the happiest of my life. I have been able to reconcile with my father and we actually enjoy tossing baseballs to each other. I recently met a wonderful woman I hope to marry. I can't wait to have my own children. I will help them find their way in this world, but it will be their way."

JOYCE: BINGE EATING AND BECOMING PREGNANT

I was surprised when Joyce entered my office for her first appointment. I had expected someone extremely overweight and depressed based on our brief initial telephone contact. On the contrary, she was only slightly overweight, seemed upbeat, certainly not depressed, and greeted me with a strong handshake.

Joyce was 34, single, an executive in a major pharmaceutical company, and she quickly took charge of our meeting. "I heard all about your unusual diet program," she began, "and I want to get started on it right away. My friend told me something about it, especially how you help people change their minds and behavior."

And so began what would turn out to be four very intense and complex sessions. Joyce was a binge eater who never attempted to throw up or use laxatives. She would go on a frighteningly exhaustive out-of-control binge followed by an equally exhaustive but highly controlled period of fasting. This sequence of binging and fasting occurred once a month and appeared related to her menstrual period. During the three or four days that the cycle ran its course she would disappear from work and social life and remain holed up in her condo accepting no calls. Her colleagues and friends believed she was just going through another of her incapacitating migraine headaches. In truth, she never suffered from headaches at all.

At first Joyce avoided telling me much about her life, claiming it had little to do with her rapid cycling binge eating as she described it. She just wanted a quick fix to stop it. It was ruining her life. She was afraid to start a relationship with a man in case her binging would be discovered. Despite her reluctance, I persuaded Joyce to briefly tell me about her life. She initially offered nothing of real help except to describe a crucial incident that occurred shortly before she started binge eating.

Until the age of eighteen her life appeared to be normal. She was a popular student, did well in her studies, was athletic, of normal weight, and never over-ate.

During her first year of college at a combined dinner between her new sorority and one of the fraternities, a number of students became sick from what was later assumed to be food poisoning. Her memory was sketchy but she recalled awakening in a hospital with an excruciating headache and connected to IV's. Her entire body was swollen double its size, she said. After several days in the hospital she was sent back to the dorm and was treated with antihistamine medication. Three weeks later she discovered she was pregnant. Against her religious beliefs she had an abortion. But the guilt and the realization she had been raped while unconscious was devastating. She told no one about the abortion. Until then she had been a virgin.

Five months after the rape she had her first love affair and said she enjoyed her first sexual experience. About a week following the sex she was surprised when her period was late. She believed she could not possibly be pregnant. She had started using the pill the previous month and her new boyfriend used a condom. She waited with rising horror as the days passed and her period had not started.

Then, as she described it, "Something broke inside me. I don't know what it was but I know that something snapped in my mind. I felt desperate and wanted to die. How could I go through another abortion? Then from nowhere I had an urge to eat. At first I did nothing. But the urge turned into something that overwhelmed me and I began to eat. I ate and I ate. I left the campus and went to a hotel. I was so embarrassed. I told everyone I was called home. Two days later while I continued to gorge myself my period came." Joyce now paused and I saw the mist appear in her eyes. She was embarrassed and tried to control the tears that slowly trickled down her face. I felt her helplessness.

I realized then that Joyce had been carrying out a monthly ritual, repeating a traumatic event in her life. But why did her fear of pregnancy take this turn? The rape and food poisoning and her swollen body, as well as her abortion, are part of it, I thought, but I felt that there was a missing link.

"I'm sorry I'm crying," she said softly, "I guess remembering when it began was too much for me."

"I can understand your reaction," I responded, "but I think you have offered a way to overcome this compulsive eating. Whatever it was that triggered your first binging episode is a good place to start trying to understand the cause and help you overcome it."

"I don't want to go back to that time. I need

something to stop it now. I came because of the mental things you do to help people."

"You're speaking of mental imagery," I said, "and I believe it can be of help. But for imagery to help you we need to find out if anything else may be contributing to your continuing binging. When she agreed to return for a second visit I suggested that she try to remember anything from her past that might be involved. Think in terms of it happening once a month that ties in with your menstrual period. Think of pregnancies, anything you might have heard or experienced in your childhood." I suggested she begin to use a journal and to write down anything pertinent.

Joyce was not as interested in losing weight as much as controlling the binging but I felt her using the entire program would help discipline her mind for what I suspected would be uncertain benefit from imagery alone. She agreed to start using water as I suggested. Her exercise routine was already excellent. Daily use of the scale and the special extra water diet were parts of the program that did interest her since she had a tendency to splurge at times and gain weight. Her motivation was high.

On her second visit Joyce reported that she had already used the extra water diet twice and it worked perfectly. She had also recalled a memory from her childhood that I felt was highly significant. Joyce was an only child and she had remembered hearing her mother tell her aunt about all the babies she had lost and how terrible she felt each time it happened. Her mother had cried when she said how sad she felt having only one child. Joyce was about six at that time.

Joyce immediately called her mother and asked

about that overheard conversation. At first her mother was reluctant to discuss it but Joyce was insistent. She learned that her mother had gone through four other pregnancies after Joyce had been born, having late miscarriages with each, until the final one which required a hysterectomy.

Joyce looked straight at me when she announced her discovery. "I asked my mother to tell me exactly what I did during her four pregnancies. At first she was hesitant to tell me any more, but I insisted. My mother told me that with each pregnancy she was so happy that I would have a brother or sister that she would pat her belly all the time and she said that she let me do the same. By the time I was three I would pat her belly and say I could feel the baby growing inside her. That's what my mother told me. That I could feel the baby inside her. After each miscarriage my mother cried and cried and she said that I did the same. I don't remember the first pregnancy. I guess I was too young, but I was aware of the next three. I was five when she had her hysterectomy."

We now had the information to work on establishing a series of imagery exercises to help Joyce overcome her binge eating. Her enthusiasm to explore every possible source of conflict and connect it to an imagery exercise was exemplary. In the remaining time of her second visit we thought up four possible imagery exercises. She decided to use two.

- The first visualization was simple but effective. Any food she brought into her condo for binging would immediately burst into flames and only when she promised herself she would never binge again would the fire go out.

- In the second imagery she created the feeling of her mother's miscarriages and her own abortion. In her imagery she gorged herself with food and watched it turn into an embryo and grow inside her. She watched her entire body grow to double its size and was terrified that she would keep growing until she exploded and the baby would be lost. She ended the imagery by saying that food is not a baby. Having a baby is wonderful. She told herself that she would never eat food to feel pregnant again.

When Joyce returned the following week she brought with her over twenty new imagery exercises that covered every conceivable aspect of binge eating. As we went over them, I realized that she was determined to conquer the binging without any formal therapy and thus the imagery would be her vehicle for getting well. We examined all her ideas and came up with a few more she decided to use as part of her daily imagery exercises. She had already established that twenty exercise periods a day was to be her schedule no matter how long each one took. Joyce was determined to get well.

Each of the imagery exercises touched on specific stress-related problems. The examples show the scope of Joyce's imagery.

- She erected a major barrier to entering the markets where she bought her binging food. As she approached the store a large crowd of hideous-looking women sprang out and pummeled her mercilessly. She begged them to stop and finally one said only when we know you will never enter a market to buy binging food again. She promised and the beating stopped. All the women who struck her were a gruesome form of herself.

- She watched as her menstrual period began and immediately felt wonderfully calm, repeating that her period no longer influenced her eating.

Without fully knowing how much stress came from her mother's reactions to the miscarriages, Joyce added another imagery exercise to the one she had started the previous week. A further discussion with her mother had revealed that her mother had gone into brief but deep depressions after each miscarriage and withdrew emotionally from Joyce. The imagery sought to correct what might have been her reaction to this information.

- Joyce visualized her mother's growing belly until it suddenly got smaller. She watched her mother break down and cry inconsolably, ignoring her daughter. Joyce screamed repeatedly at her for being a bad mommy who was more concerned with a dead baby than with her. Not until her mother apologized for withdrawing from her and assured Joyce she loved her very much did Joyce stop her screaming and forgive her mother.

This was a particularly difficult exercise for Joyce because it meant facing the anger she must have felt as a small child when her mother withdrew from her. Her imagery really took the place of much of what therapy would have done. It gave her insight into the underlying aspects of her compulsive eating. Her last exercise was end-state imagery.

- She saw herself watching the days on the calendar as her menstrual period came and went and knew that she no longer binged. Her binging days were finally over. She felt joy and a renewed sense of self-control. She also saw herself having reached her desired weight. She saw herself laughing and happy knowing her life had changed and she had gained full control of herself.

Joyce added these exercises to the first two. At her fourth and final visit she brought in another dozen or so imagery exercises to show me the direction of her thinking. I told her that she should make her own selections now and to continually update and add new imagery as needed. She should also continue to look for other conflicts that affected her eating or her self-image. She assured me that she would follow the full diet program despite only needing to lose 10 or 15 pounds. Finally, she smiled warmly as she told me that she knew her life was about to change.

I didn't hear from Joyce again until two years later when she sent me a brief note and her wedding picture. Joyce looked beautiful and serene standing next to her new husband. Their mutual joy was very evident.

A year and a half after that I received my last letter and another picture from her; the picture of a beautiful seven-pound baby girl. Joyce ended her letter saying that she named the baby after her mother.

JESSICA: BODY IMAGE AND THE COMPULSION TO EAT

"Doctor, you must help me lose all this fat right now," were the first words I heard from the attractive young woman sitting in my office. "I look just terrible and I hate myself."

Jessica was just 26 years old and suffering from a common problem of body image distortion. At 5' 6" and weighing only 148 pounds one could scarcely call her fat and some would not even call her overweight. But Jessica felt huge and out of control and desperately wanted to lose weight.

Since the age of 15 she had felt fat. Due to innumerable diets, her weight had fluctuated from 125 to 150 pounds. She went through starvation periods, drinking only tea for five days at a time, eating only bananas, using any diets in vogue, and taking a variety of diet medications, some of which caused severe nausea that she said helped her lose weight. But nothing worked for long. She would go on two or three diets a year. "I've tried everything. Nobody wants to lose weight as much as I do. But even when I manage to lose it I just can't keep it off."

Although she lost varying amounts of weight on all of the diets, she rapidly regained her weight when her interest in the diet waned, which usually happened within a few weeks. Her compulsive need to eat overwhelmed her most strenuous efforts to diet.

Her background was significant. There were a large

number of obese or extremely overweight members in her family. Both of her parents, two of her three siblings, and various uncles, aunts and cousins were heavy. However, her idea of being overweight was ten or fifteen pounds over normal weight. Her ideal figure was tied to the images of very thin models and movie stars.

Jessica ate small amounts of food all day long. She could not stop her compulsion to eat whenever food appeared in front of her. There was no pattern and no particular food. Anything would do and at any time. Every bite brought more self-loathing and feelings of ugliness, which intensified her urge to eat. Jessica had developed a vicious cycle. Compulsive eating leading to self-condemnation causing compulsive eating, and so on.

Diets rarely work with people like Jessica until they find a way to change their belief systems attached to their eating compulsion. It is often difficult to convince them of the need to use psychological tools such as mental imagery before starting their diet. They are so unhappy about their weight that unless they are given a program to lose weight quickly they aren't interested. Unless Jessica could understand the value of changing her thinking patterns, another failure would occur and her self-esteem would again collapse.

"Jessica," I began, "are you open to trying a brand new approach to dieting that is different from all those you've tried?"

"I'll do anything you say," she quickly answered.

"I appreciate your confidence in me," I replied, "but I believe that to help you, which I will make every effort to do, we need to collaborate on a method that will offer you something that you haven't yet tried. Dieting is hard for many people and we need to find out what your specific problems are."

For a few moments Jessica looked at me, not yet comprehending that she would become a participant in establishing her diet program. "What do you mean, we collaborate. Of course, I'll do whatever you say."

I carefully described how her mind has gained control over her eating behavior and we have to find a way of changing whatever thoughts, ideas, or beliefs she has that are making her eat compulsively.

"Yes, I know what you mean. Even when I want to stop eating I don't seem to be able to do it."

"Right," I said, "that's it. You have some negative beliefs that cause you to eat even when it makes you so unhappy."

"Sometimes I want to shut my mind off," she exclaimed. "Sometimes I feel like cutting my head off so I won't eat and I won't hear that voice saying it's okay to eat."

I smiled inwardly. In a few sentences Jessica had provided the ideas for her first imagery exercises. "Yes, just imagine if you could actually shut down your mind or change those thoughts that make you eat, you could then walk away from food."

Jessica had quickly realized that her mind had opposing thoughts. One said, "Eat." The other said, "Don't eat." The "eat" thoughts were more powerful and won most of the battles and when they did Jessica experienced intense guilt since her "don't eat" side punished her. I explained this dichotomy of her mind and she immediately grasped it.

"The 'eat' part we call a negative belief system.

However, because the 'don't eat' part caused you to hate yourself, that is also a negative belief."

"I get it," she almost screamed. "I can't win this battle because I have nothing inside my head that is really working for me. Nothing is helping."

"Then, how about if you and I work out a way to change these negative beliefs and finally give your mind new beliefs that will help you stop overeating?" I asked.

"I want to do it. I know I can change my mind if I know how to do it."

"Jessica, there is a way that works if you're willing to give it time. Changing beliefs is not easy and requires persistence and continual daily exercises." I then told her about how mental imagery works, especially emphasizing how actresses and athletes use it to foster improvement in their professional and personal lives.

I explained that she needed to do the imagery for a minimum of one month, every day with absolute enthusiasm and belief in its effectiveness. At that point she'd begin her actual diet. "Autosuggestion is your tool to changing your thinking. But it needs much repetition. Do you think you can put all your energy into the imagery and not feel you're being deprived of the actual diet program for a month?" I asked.

Jessica reflected on my question. "I want to lose weight so badly that I may have trouble not actually dieting, but nothing has ever worked and I understand how my mind stops me from losing weight. I'll do it the way you say."

Jessica became like an athlete striving for perfection. She practiced the imagery exercises up to 30 times a day. My primary concern was whether she'd stick with it long enough to make it effective. The early imagery was primed to maintain her motivation as well as prepare her to control her eating. In the first two sessions she created ten imagery exercises that she used repeatedly in her imagery sessions. Following is a brief description of the exercises she used.

- She was in a straitjacket unable to move her arms or legs. Mountains of food that she could no longer reach surrounded her. She told herself that she would never lift a finger to touch forbidden foods again. She was forever free of overeating.
- She grabbed food from a table, stuffing it into her mouth and watching herself become immensely fat. She gazed in horror at what she did to herself and swore she would never do it again.
- She put chains and locks on refrigerators and cupboards so that she couldn't get to the food.
- She took food from a friend and a policeman came over and hauled her off to jail for doing harm to herself.
- She stuffed food down her throat and saw all her hair fall out and her skin wrinkle as she grew old, fat, and ugly.
- She visualized tables filled with food and washing it away with a fire hose. She exulted in her ability to keep her hands off of the food. She knew she had conquered her compulsive eating.

- She saw herself as enormous and grotesque. No one would come near her. She was absolutely repulsive. With a determined voice she said, "That is the old me." She then put a large box over that version of herself and replaced it with a beautiful body weighing 125 pounds, her ideal weight. She hugged her new self. She repeated many times that she would always love herself and never damage her body with excess weight gain.
- She visualized herself as a beautiful, energetic, and appealing woman at the end of her diet. She knew for certain that her wonderful body was consistent with her body build. She used this imagery in a variety of guises, either strolling on the beach in a bikini or wearing a trim skirt and blouse and attracting the attention of men and women.

The imagery exercises that Jessica used were all simple but effective. Each dieter must determine what seems suitable and then use the imagery with highly charged emotions. Jessica exaggerated each exercise. For example, when the cop came to take her to jail she threw up all over him and herself and saw terrible boils appear on her body. The imagery was simple but the effect was dramatic. The mind always knows the intent of the imagery and is influenced by intensity, which is why you should exaggerate it. The power is in the feelings. The more intense the more effective.

At the end of the concentrated month of imagery exercises Jessica surprised me by saying she had lost seven pounds without trying to diet. Apparently, within days after starting the imagery she became increasingly disgusted by her constant snacking and actually began to feel sick whenever she reached for food. During the second half of the month she totally stopped all nibbling and limited herself to three small meals a day which she enjoyed.

After congratulating her on the rapid change in her thinking about eating and her weight loss, I indicated that she needed to continue the imagery for a number of months. A major dilemma had arisen, which I fully discussed with her. Her pattern with past diet programs was to lose weight rapidly. The same thing had occurred with her new diet, although only the imagery part of the diet was used. Jessica was highly suggestible, which partly explains why she could quickly lose weight with any program. However, she needed to find a way to establish permanent weight control.

I now had to introduce the stabilization period. My explanation of the other elements in the program were immediately understood but my emphasis on now stabilizing her seven-pound weight loss was hard for her to grasp. She felt she was "on a roll" and wanted to continue losing weight. Convincing her to now stop losing weight for one month was going to be a challenge. But unless she could learn to control her weight-loss and not reduce her metabolism, I believed that the probability of ultimately failing her new diet was high. I carefully explained all this to her.

"You don't understand, doctor. I did exactly what you told me and I already lost seven pounds. The imagery is wonderful and I no longer have any desire to eat all that fattening food."

"In the other 20 or 30 diets you tried did you have

any trouble losing weight?" I asked.

"No, I already told you that. I could always lose weight easily."

"Jessica, that's the point. You did the same with my diet. Although you were only working with imagery, you practically stopped eating. Your ability to quickly gain control over your eating is commendable but now you have to prove to yourself that it's permanent. Isn't that what you want?" I asked looking directly into her eyes.

Jessica looked down and was silent for several minutes. Finally she spoke. "You're right. I have felt this control before for short periods. It does feel very different now but how do I really know that I won't immediately regain all the weight? I'll follow your diet the way you think is best for me."

Jessica faithfully followed the program and continued to use the imagery. She slowly developed the certainty of her newfound control. At my suggestion she slowed down her monthly weight loss and required nine months to reach 125 pounds. She came to see me every other month during that period. On her last visit I saw a young woman of true inner and outer beauty. Her confidence and self-esteem shone in her face and bearing. Although I did not hear from her again, I have little doubt that she had mastered the inner control she had sought.

RICHARD: MOTIVATION AND CHANGING BELIEFS

Richard, a 54-year-old moderately obese man and an accountant by profession, came to see me "to go on my last diet," he laughingly remarked. "My buddy,

Greg, who you helped, told me to see you. He said you have a whole bag of tricks up your sleeve for guys like me."

Richard did not appear unduly disturbed by his weight. At 5' 7" he weighed about 190 pounds and commented that's where he remains stuck despite having dieted over a hundred times. He had been able to get down to 170 pounds three or four times. But in a relatively short time he regained his lost weight. He had no knowledge of imagery or stabilization and deliberately never stepped on a scale. His exercise was irregular, although he played tennis occasionally.

During the first visit he tended to joke a bit about his condition and that his wife liked to tickle his fat belly. His two teenage children were both normal weight but his 45-year-old wife was on the "heavy" side. "We rub our fat together and that's really a turn on," he laughed.

He said his wife was about twenty pounds overweight and she was also interested in dieting. She was currently going to Weight Watchers and seemed satisfied with maintaining her current weight. He admitted grudgingly that his wife at times did frown on his excessive eating and drinking but, he reassured me, "she's really a good sport and doesn't mind my being a little heavy."

On close questioning it became apparent that fast food, candy bars, three or four beers a night, and a big juicy steak were par for the course. In describing his eating habits he made no reference to the unhealthy nature of his diet. Vegetables and fruits were not part of his regular diet except for an apple now and then.

His motivation was the success of his friend who

essentially cajoled him into seeing me. The need to set Richard on a path toward dietary and weight control now depended on his conversion to becoming a health-minded and self-directed dieter. After determining that there appeared to be no major genetic or medical factors contributing to his obesity and no obvious emotional conflicts that might interfere with his diet, I set my sights on encouraging him to see the value in losing weight and maintaining it.

Unless Richard developed a greater desire to lose weight and was willing to change his dietary habits I doubted his motivation was sufficient to carry him through the year or more it would take to lose 30 or 40 pounds. His previous diets were all established with fast-acting drugs or rapid weight-loss techniques. Those diets barely lasted a month before he gave up and was quickly back to his old weight.

During his first visit when I obtained his history and described the diet program, Richard seemed ready and willing to go ahead. I said nothing about changing to a healthier diet. Despite my suggesting he might want to take notes as I described the program, he assured me he'd remember everything I told him.

Many patients hide their real feelings about their body and mental attitudes. They fear revealing what might not be changeable and, by covering up conflicts and doubts, avoid facing issues that ultimately sabotage their efforts to lose weight. Did Richard's joking and playful banter hide some fear? Did he really come here only because his friend persuaded him? Why had he only tried short quick diets even though he had learned they never worked? Such questions needed answering.

One week later he appeared twenty minutes late offering the excuse of traffic delays. He started the session by telling me a rather crude joke. Thus I was warned that not much had changed in the past week. On questioning I learned that he tried to drink more water a few times but he couldn't figure out why drinking so much water would help him when he already drank five or six cups of coffee, a half dozen soft drinks, and three or four beers a day. He had forgotten my previous explanation of why plain water was needed and not just other liquids containing water. He said that his scale was broken and he had no time to buy a new one. He also admitted that his exercise routine had not changed.

My work was laid out for me. He needed to be motivated to really want to lose weight. It was clear that something was frightening Richard. He didn't call to cancel his session with me as he could have. "Richard," I said, "I know that you would like to lose weight or you wouldn't be here, but something is bothering you and keeping you from wanting to start a new diet. What is it?"

At first he only grunted a few denials. On further questioning he admitted that he doubted he had the staying power to diet. Finally, he told me his deeper fear. "Doc, I think I may have heart trouble." He had developed chest pain on mild exercising during the past three or four months. He had become afraid of having sex and had become impotent. His wife accused him of not loving her anymore. He had withdrawn into gambling to occupy his mind.

While in my office I insisted he call his family doctor and make an appointment for an immediate physical examination, which he did. His examination was scheduled for the following day. We then discussed how his fear had thwarted his judgment. He needed to change his lifestyle, lose weight, and develop more confidence in his ability to control his life. Behind his façade of humor was a frightened, lost soul. His willingness to divulge his fears augured well for developing the proper motivation to diet. I then encouraged him to copy down my directions for the program and to begin a journal and write down his fears and doubts and what he eats. He agreed to do it and said, "I'll buy a scale today and start weighing myself."

Richard did not have heart disease. He suffered from anxiety manifested by chest pain and palpitations. His symptoms were related to a fear of growing old, losing his sexual potency, and believing (wrongly as it turned out) that his wife had become disgusted with him. On probing, it became clear that he knew he was harvesting his own fears of an early death with his unhealthy diet and lack of exercise. It turned out his tennis was so infrequent he didn't remember the last time he played. Knowing that he could quickly lose motivation I introduced him to mental imagery. I explained its value in helping him lose weight and, perhaps even more important, in helping him overcome his doubts about his sexuality, physical fitness, and general lifestyle. He would start the imagery the following session.

By his third visit Richard was ready to begin the use of mental imagery. He practiced the rag doll technique in my office a few times and was surprised how relaxed it made him feel. He immediately recognized the value of imagery and was eager to apply it to his life. He started with the end-state imagery.

- He imagined himself at a reasonable weight, in good health, walking swiftly, playing singles tennis, and making vigorous love.

The second imagery exercise was developed to stop his raiding the refrigerator for food.

- He visualized an electric field around the refrigerator. Whenever he reached to open the refrigerator door or even approach it he was shocked. By his fourth or fifth repetition of the imagery the shock had become so intense it threw him across the room. He swore he would never open the refrigerator door for food to overeat.

The third imagery was especially meaningful to him because he created it out of his compulsive urge to go to fast food restaurants whenever he felt the slightest urge to eat. Richard created this imagery without my help after we had discussed where, how, and when he overate.

- Around McDonald's, Wendy's, and Jack-in-the-Box, all his favorites, he saw enormous hamburgers, twenty feet high, holding big clubs ready to smash his head in if he got close to them. There were large amounts of fries running up and down in front of the burgers, all covered with long thorns and spines, threatening to scratch his eyes out if he dared touch them. Leading the fries was a huge coke twirling its straw and whistling a funeral march.

Richard broke out into gales of laughter at his amazing creation, as he termed it. He had become a mental imagery devotee in one brief session.

During the next month Richard learned about nutritious dieting. He decided to try his hand at cooking, which became a new hobby. He cooked only healthy foods. He learned that vegetables and fruits and low fat foods were, in fact, delicious. The stabilization period made immediate sense to him and, for the first time, he found he could indeed stabilize his weight. He also understood how losing weight slowly offers a chance for the body and mind to accommodate to it. He regained sexual potency very quickly and in several intimate conversations with his wife was able to discuss his fears about their relationship deteriorating.

Richard cried for the first and only time in my office when he told me how wrong he had been about his wife's feelings. She had felt he was withdrawing from her and, unable to understand why or find an opening to discuss her feelings with him, she too had withdrawn. When they perceived how their distorted reactions almost caused a major breach in their love for each other, they both cried unashamedly together. Richard was on the way to establishing a completely new lifestyle.

By his seventh and last visit with me Richard had become devoted to sustaining a healthy and vital life. I had no doubt that he was now on a lifelong path to much more than permanent weight control. Richard was on his way to making his dreams of becoming more loving and more creative a reality. I shared his pleasure as he described how he created his imagery exercises at home. At times he would bring his journal to read to me about the dreams or fantasies he had that gave him new insights. During his last visit he emphasized that the stabilization period did more than help him learn how to control his weight. It gave him the inner strength to control his life. The creation of his imagery had gone far beyond his dieting because now he used it to overcome anxiety about public speaking and to improve his tennis. He was now playing singles on a weekly schedule.

Richard had fought hard to change his beliefs. He was willing to look into himself and know that he was not what he wanted to be. And he found the way to change.

A year and a half after I last saw Richard he wrote me his final letter to tell me that he has weighed 150 pounds for the past four months and weight control is now part of his permanent thinking. His continuing use of water is automatic and he never forgets to step on the scale each morning. Each morning he rises feeling buoyant and alive. Before breakfast he uses a new imagery exercise as a reminder that he should never take his weight control for granted. It's one that you might like to try.

"When I close my eyes while deeply relaxed I imagine that I'm flying high in the sky, floating over great canyons and lakes and majestic trees. I am thrilled with the sight below me and elated by my ability to fly. Suddenly, I sink to the ground. I am unable to rise and I know that I have gained weight. I can no longer fly. I promise myself that I'll always respect my body and never burden it with extra weight. And with those thoughts, the extra weight disappears, and I again fly into the air. This time I'm accompanied by hundreds of birds and butterflies. I am uplifted and thank myself for saving my life."

The imagery takes less than a minute to do, Richard informed me and "I'm always surprised at the many different places I'm able to view from high in the sky." Richard has opened his eyes to a new world which, as he fully knows, represents his world within.

Entering the world of Richard and my other patients as they struggled to find new directions and meaning in their lives gave me much insight into the ways we seek understanding and personal growth. You have read this book hoping to find a new and effective way to lose weight and not regain it. You now know that I don't espouse quick weight loss or special diets. I emphasize changing your thinking and changing yourself.

All five keys to permanent weight loss are connected to changing your beliefs about dieting. Any of them will be helpful. All together they become powerful instruments in your mental toolbox for making your life healthier and happier.

Eating is a necessary part of life. We just can't say we won't eat. The question becomes how do you eat to satisfy your hunger and need for nutrition and not compromise your health or self-esteem.

We share a common goal. I want to help you overcome a compulsive overeating habit and find new ways to make your life better and happier. I'm sure you want the same for yourself. I know this program will work. The basis for its effectiveness has been documented over many years. I want you to believe that you can incorporate it and use it and enjoy it. I especially want you to believe in yourself. Believe in your empowerment to change your life. That is your personal key to your future. Believing in your ability to change and grow is what keeps you forever young and alive. Achieving permanent weight control is just the beginning of changing your life.

INDEX

About the Author

Marvin H. Berenson, M.D. is Clinical Professor of Psychiatry and Behavioral Sciences at the University of Southern California School of Medicine and specializes in the use of mental imagery for the treatment of psychosomatic disorders, addictions, compulsive disorders, and weight control problems.

He uses a diverse array of psychological techniques in his general clinical work that include psychoanalysis, behavioral and cognitive therapy, as well as guided imagery therapy.

Early in his clinical practice he created a series of mental imagery techniques and exercises that he used to enhance creativity, improve artistic and literary skills, help athletes maximize their performances, and treat various physical and emotional problems. From these early beginnings he soon developed the entire program for aiding overweight people to finally lose weight and maintain permanent weight control.

Dr. Berenson is a member of the American Psychoanalytic Association, the International Psychoanalytic Association, the American Psychiatric Association, and the Alpha Omega Alpha Honorary Medical Society.